A FEW OF ROXIE'S WOOF-WORTHY THOUGHTS

The worker put me back in the puppy room crate. I noticed my crate now had ADOPTED on it. I did not understand. The door to the room closed. I fell fast asleep still smelling the scent of the man's nose nuzzle. Where did he go? Would I see him again? (See Story #4)

By the way, I quickly learned about "biscuit." I still will do most anything to get a little biscuit. Steve calls me a "biscuit tart." I think that is a good thing. (See Story #7)

Where did he go? I didn't see him anymore. I just sat there, like Steve told me to do. But I tell you, I did not like it. It felt like the night in the box when that person left me on the side of the road. Was Steve leaving me, too? I didn't understand this. My heart beat a little faster. (See Story #10)

I thought, if all human beings treated each other with the same dignity as expected of us dogs and their people, what a wonderful world it must be. (See Story #13)

"I just learned I have a brain tumor." She kept contact with my back. She and Steve spoke, though she did most of the speaking in a soft voice. I listened. It sounded like she was sad. And her hand never left my back. I continued to lean into her. (See Story #21)

I watch other dogs run, jump, and dig. They look like they are having fun. I lay there. Some might call me lazy. I prefer to call it economy of motion. (See Story #24)

On that day in the parking lot, Steve had made a mistake and he learned a valuable lesson. He never made that mistake again. I am glad that he pays attention and is a quick study. (See Story #29)

One of Steve's t-shirts displays these words: "Dogs speak but only to those who know how to listen." Sounds simple to me. Why would anyone want to speak to someone who will not listen? (See Story #30)

As Steve pulls, the rope will slip bit by bit from my jaws. But when I reach that knot, I get a better grip and dig in with all my might. I feel more in control. I feel strong! All because of a knot at the end of my rope. This helps me gather myself…The knot at the end of my rope. Everyone could use one. (See Story #37)

That reminded me how fortunate I have been. From the person who found me on the side of that road at the beginning of my story to my "Gotcha Day" to where I sit today, I have had more cheerleaders than I can count on my paws and dewclaws. (See Story #42)

People often ask Steve how long it took to train me. I really do not like that word, train. You train a seal. You bond with your dog. IMHCO—In My Humble Canine Opinion. (See Story #51)

As Steve and I sat on the sand and watched the sun rise over the water, a neighbor approached and said hello. She looked at me stretched out on the cool soft beach. She smiled, and said, "It's a good day to be dog." And then she added, "Every day's a good day to be a dog." Steve smiled and said, "Especially if there are good people in that dog's life." (See Story #52)

Roxie Looks for Purpose Beyond the Biscuit

For Faith!

Roxie & *Steve*

"WOOF!"

Roxie (The Dog)

with

Steve Piscitelli (Her Person)

ISBN: 978-0-9982585-2-2

First Edition

Also, by Steve Piscitelli

Community as a Safe Place to Land
*Stories about Teaching, Learning, and Resilience:
No Need to be an Island*
Choices for College Success, 3rd edition
Study Skills: Do I Really Need This Stuff? 3rd edition
Engaging Activities for Student Success
*I Don't Need This Stuff! Or Do I? A Study Skills and
Time Management Book*
*Does Anyone Understand This Stuff?
A Student Guide to Organizing United States History, 2nd edition*

DEDICATION

From Roxie:

To rescued and to-be rescued canines.
May you be blessed with caring humans and a biscuit
or two along your journey.
AND
To Maker's. One of the first canine friends I met on the beach.
I look forward to seeing you over the Rainbow Bridge.

From Steve:

To our pet therapy mentors who have guided, shared, loved,
and taught Roxie and me how to
lean in, listen, and learn.

CONTENTS

GRATITUDE

A lot of people have helped us (Roxie and Steve) conceive, carry, and deliver this book to and for you. Not by writing the book. Not by sponsoring the book. In fact, most have not even seen the manuscript. These people have supported us as a team. They have encouraged us. They have challenged us. They have taught us.

All of their combined kindness and insights have helped us develop into the partnership we have become. A wag of the tail and a hearty "WOOF!" go out to each and every one of you.

Steve has shared with me that most GRATITUDE sections come up short. While well-meaning, they miss people. Both Steve and I remain indebted to so many (humans and canines) we have met along our journey. You know who you are. If we have not listed you, please know that is our shortcoming and not yours. After all, Steve is getting forgetful, and I might get distracted at times by the thought of a biscuit. Just saying!

Ear scratches, belly rubs, and biscuits to all of the following (in alphabetical order):

Amy Judd, Anne Bell, Ashli Archer, Atlantic Beach (Florida) Elementary School, Baptist Medical Center Beaches (nurses, staff, patients, volunteers, and family members), Kim Gallagher, JAXPaws at Jacksonville International Airport, Laurie Piscitelli, Marcie Ryan, Penny Moran, Pooches' Playhouse, San Pablo

Animal Clinic, Sandy Golding, Stacy Strickland, the Alliance of Therapy Dogs, the Jacksonville Humane Society, the Ruffarees and crew at Brewhound, the Sixth Street (Atlantic Beach, Florida) Dogs, and Therapy Animal Coalition.

Roxie and Steve

ABOUT ROXIE

Hi, **I'm Roxie.** I am what people call a rescue dog. My person, Steve, adopted me from the Jacksonville Humane Society (JHS) in July of 2015. I live with him and his wife, Hoppi (whose real name is Laurie. You will learn how Steve loves nicknames.).

The JHS estimated me to be fourteen weeks old when Steve and I met. My papers say I am a Labrador Retriever mix. I have been "fixed" so I cannot have pups of my own. Depending on how the light hits my fur, I look either black or chocolate brown.

Steve and I have been a pet therapy team since 2018. We live in Atlantic Beach, Florida.

I have a blog at https://roxiebeyondthebiscuit.home.blog/. My Instagram "handle" is *beyondthebiscuit*.

This is my first book. Thank goodness Steve knows how to type.

ABOUT STEVE

Hi, I'm Steve. Some people call me *Roxie's Owner*. I'm not fond of that. Others refer to me as *Roxie's Person*. I like that better, as she deserves top billing. More than anything, we are *Partners*. We have become a nationally-certified pet therapy team. We visit the hospital in our community, the airport, and local schools to provide comfort and support as needed.

It is a lucky thing that I retired from classroom teaching in 2015, as Roxie keeps me busy with our pet therapy rounds. She does give me time to speak, write, record, and volunteer in my community.

Thank goodness for Roxie. Without her, there is no story to tell.

You can learn more about us at www.stevepiscitelli.com.

I AM THE "LDE"— LUCKIEST DOG EVER!

WHO HAS BLESSED YOUR LIFE?

Hi, I'm Roxie. A dog. This is my story or, at least, a piece of it. When the story started, I didn't have much going for me. You see, I was abandoned on the side of a road. I am not sure why or by whom. I don't remember much about my mother. I don't know when I was born. That person who left me must have known someone would help me. And someone did. In fact, more than one human has blessed my life.

I ended up in a place where a lot of other dogs, like me and unlike me, were being cared for. The man examining me was not sure what I was. He looked at my toes, my snout, and head. He looked me up and down. I heard him say, before he put me in a crate, "This one is a lab mix. About fourteen weeks."

Not sure what it meant.

I am a lucky pup. I have people who love me and care for me. Some call me "BDE"—Best Dog Ever.

I'm not sure about that. I'm just a dog. I like all other beings. I think I am "LDE"—the Luckiest Dog Ever.

Anyway, thank you for picking up my first book and reading about my journey. The short stories in the following pages share life as I see it from my paws and through my eyes. You will read of lessons I learned about obstacles, fears, respect, curiosity, companionship, and quiet time. Hopefully, my observations will help you on your journey.

One note. I'm still not good at typing. All paw pads and dew-claws, if you get the picture. And I don't speak any human language. Now, you might consider that a drawback when writing a book, but I have had help. My person, Steve, has done his best to capture my thoughts, fears, joys, and lessons. I have faith in him as he has come a long way since we first met. So, these stories represent the best of our collaborations. If there are any errors, I will take responsibility as Steve, after all, continues to be a work in progress. He's my person, and I stand by him.

Woof!

-Roxie

Contact Information

I would love to hear from you. Let me know what you find of interest in my stories and what other topics you would like for me to woof about. Contact me at roxiesperson@gmail.com. My person, Steve, will relay your message to me.

A WORD ABOUT PURPOSE

WHY SHOULD YOU CARE ABOUT THIS BOOK?

I hear Steve often use the word *purpose*. He does not like to do things just to do them or because he was told to do them. He always asks *why*? He wants to know the meaning behind his actions. The more I am with him the more I believe this motivates him more than anything.

Purpose serves Steve like biscuits serve me.

If there is purpose waiting at the end of the line, he is all in. If he had one, he'd wag his tail when he does something that serves a higher purpose.

Before I came to live with Steve, I hear he taught school for a long time—especially if you counted it in dog years. He enjoyed working with his students and helping them find their purpose. He asked—and still does today—a lot of questions. A. Lot. Of. Questions.

Purpose and questions.

So, that led me to think about this book. What or who does it serve? Why should you care about this book? After all, I'm a dog. Why read it? Why recommend it to your friends and family?

I believe that Steve and I found each other for a greater reason than giving me a place to sleep and eat. As the relationship I have with Steve continues to develop so does our purpose. It continues to evolve as I believe it does for all of us—canines and humans. I hope my stories and insights will encourage you to ask deeper questions about your stories and your purpose for being.

We all have stories we tell ourselves. And, then, there are the stories we live.

Why do you do what you do? Who or what higher meaning does it serve?

Steve kids me that, with my nose to the ground, I'm always looking for a lost scone or hidden biscuit. He calls me a "Biscuit Tart."

"You'll do anything for a biscuit, Roxie, won't you?"

While that is partly true, there is something much deeper that I am still teaching Steve about.

We all must learn to move *beyond the biscuit*—beyond immediate gratification—and discover the clues, lessons, and growth opportunities that surround us. To do that, though, we must pay attention.

Every time I smell, stare at, or paw something, there is a reason. In part, this book will allow *you* to pause and reflect on *your* moments. And, in pausing, I hope that my simple stories will motivate you to take the time to reflect on your purpose. Toward that end, each of the following short stories will conclude with the section *Beyond the Biscuit*. You will find questions to help you consider the who, what, why, and where of your purpose.

As Steve tells me, I am a work in progress.

And so is he.

And so are you.

Here's to all of us as we move beyond the biscuit.

ABANDONMENT AND FORWARD MOVEMENT

HAVE YOU EVER FELT AS IF YOU WERE ALONE AND LEFT IN THE DARK?

I was groggy. My memory a bit of a blur. A pair of soft, fleshy hands around my belly. Though I felt a rhythmic swaying, my legs did not move. Through half-closed eyes I could make out lights coming and going above me.

Just a few hours earlier I remembered moving in the opposite direction—same lights whirring overhead. Now, I did not feel quite as alert.

Lights. I remembered lights a few days back, but I was somewhere else. I don't know where, specifically. I remember a box. Big enough for me to stretch out on the bottom. I heard something slam and, suddenly, a rumble came from under the box. I felt forward movement. The movement and the rumble lulled me to sleep. Or maybe it was the hunger. I had not had much to eat that day.

Next thing I knew, the rumbling stopped. I could feel the box and me being lifted upward. I saw a person, but I could not make out the face in the dark. I felt water. I think it fell from the person's face.

As the person walked, holding me and the box, I heard the crunching of leaves and sticks. After a while, we stopped, and the box was placed ever-so-gently on the ground. The person leaned in, moved a soft cloth around my body. I felt a stroke on my head. Then nothing.

I heard crunching again, and soon it faded.

Silence. And noise.

Lots of motors, screeching, and honking. I was not sure what was happening. I curled up tightly in the corner of the box with the towel and fell asleep.

I kind of remember the box being picked up, again. An anonymous face peering in and saying, "Poor puppy. Who would leave you on the side of a road?" I looked up and I felt my little tail anxiously thump against the box.

Slam. Rumble. Forward Movement. Sleep.

Next morning, when I opened my eyes I was in a crate. Surrounded by other crates. Lots of small puppies about my size. Every so often the door to the room would open. Then a puppy would be removed from a cage.

I watched wide-eyed. One at a time they would leave. A while later they'd be back. Asleep, I think. Limp. Gently placed back in the crate by a human.

Best I can tell I was the last one of the puppies to be taken. As I left the room in a human's arms, I noticed all the other crates had something on them. All the same.

ADOPTED.

Nothing on my crate. As I would later learn, that would lead to more forward movement for me.

Beyond the Biscuit

Have you ever felt as if you were alone and left in the dark? How did you find your way? What and/or who helped you move forward? How did this help you become the person you are today?

NOSE NUZZLE

WHERE DID HE GO? WOULD I SEE HIM AGAIN?

Groggy and squinty-eyed, I lay splayed out on the cold crate floor. Around me I heard puppies whimpering and, some, barking. "Where did they get the energy to bark?" I thought. All I could muster was to lean the side of my head against the crate door and doze.

I lost track of time. I fell in and out sleep. I dreamed of the box, the rumble, the humans, the water falling on me. And then all the puppies barked in unison. So loud it made me jump. That was the first time I felt the hurt down on my belly.

Whoa! That smarts.

The room's door swung inward. A man and a woman walked in with the human who had been tending to me in the crate.

"What's wrong with this one?" asked the man as he pointed toward me. "It's the only one without an ADOPTED sign."

Through glassy eyes, I could see him point and peer in at me. He had a kind face.

"She just came back from surgery. She's been spayed. So, no one has seen her yet, except you."

They spoke some more and then my crate door opened, and two soft, gentle hands picked me up. I was carried out of the room, down the hall, and into a small room. There were no crates or puppies in this room. The man and woman followed.

"How will she behave when the drugs wear off?" The man now was holding me and looking into my eyes. He placed me on his legs and gently stroked my back. It felt good. I placed my head down on one of his hands. "Can we come back tomorrow to check on this little one once she is herself?"

He picked me up, holding me under my front legs, and brought his face close to mine. He smiled and nuzzled his nose to mine. It felt good. Really good.

The worker took me. They talked some more. I heard "tomorrow" again. Was that my name? I didn't care.

The worker put me back in the puppy room crate. I noticed my crate now had ADOPTED on it. I did not understand. The door to the room closed. I fell fast asleep still smelling the scent of the man's nose nuzzle.

Where did he go? Would I see him again?

Beyond the Biscuit

At times, "today" can be challenging, and we wish for "tomorrow" to get here quickly. But it seems so far away. Maybe you wanted to be chosen for a team, a job, or a special project, but it did not happen. Or, at least, it did not happen as quickly as you had hoped. How did you choose to respond? How did you grow from that experience? Finally, what suggestion would you give to a friend who anxiously waits for good news to come his or her way?

GOTCHA DAY

WHO HAS BEEN YOUR "TOMORROW MAN OR WOMAN"—A PERSON WHO CAME TO YOUR "RESCUE" AT A PIVOTAL POINT IN YOUR LIFE?

I awakened the next morning, still a bit sore but less groggy. I peered out the metal crate door. While I could not see my neighbors, I could hear some barking. And I smelled odors. Dog odors, I guess. I sniffed my crate. No pee or pooh on my part.

As I lay on my belly, front legs extended forward, my head on my paws, I thought it must've been a dream. Did a man really hold me? And what was that word? Tomorrow? Yeah, that was it. Tomorrow. But what did it mean?

I took a deep breath, held it shortly, and then let it go.

Harrumph!

Time for a nap.

Next thing I heard was the crate door opening. A smiling human looked in.

"Hi, puppy! I think we have found you a home." With cupped hands, she scooped me up and carried me to the small room I visited briefly the day before. As we entered, I caught a familiar scent. And then she handed me to a man. It was the "Tomorrow Man!" He took me and held me to his face and nose nuzzled me again.

"Well, she still seems calm. Is she still sedated?"

"No, the drugs wore off during the night. She's probably still a little sore. But what you see is undrugged!"

"I like her. Can we take her home today?"

And with that tomorrow became today.

Papers were signed. The man carried me to his car and placed me on the woman's lap. I later learned that she was his wife. She felt good and had a nice smell.

Another rumble came from below. Forward movement, again. I fell asleep.

_____

Beyond the Biscuit

Who has been your "tomorrow man or woman"—a person who came to your rescue at a pivotal point in your life? Perhaps it was a mentor, a teacher, a coach, a friend, a boss, a spiritual leader, or a family member. What did this person do to help and guide you? How has this shaped your life?

QUIET EXPLORATION

WHEN DID YOU FACE AN OBSTACLE THAT SEEMED INSURMOUNTABLE? HOW DID YOU MOVE FORWARD?

To this point, I had been surrounded by noise. Speeding cars and honking horns filled the box that cradled me that night on the side of the road. The puppy room always had whimpers and barks bouncing off the tiled walls and concrete floors.

And now, quiet. The man, who I gathered was known as Steve, and the woman, Hoppi, stopped the car. I was still in Hoppi's lap, but my nose was up. Sniffing.

Where was I? Would I be left someplace again? Another crate? More noise?

She opened the car door and stepped out with me. We were in front of a brown building that did not look anything like the puppy room building. It was smaller and seemed happy with all the colors surrounding it.

"Welcome home," said Hoppi as she followed Steve through a gate on the side of the building.

Home? Was that my name?

We walked down a small pathway, and then I was put down on the ground. I just sat there and looked around. I'd never seen anything so open, green, and soft. No cars. No puppies. Just me, Steve, and Hoppi.

"Come, Roxie! Come!" Steve said.

Roxie? What is a Roxie? I turned my head to see.

I got up, sniffed the ground, walked a few steps, squatted, and peed.

"Good girl, Roxie! Good girl!" He came over and stroked my head gently. It felt good. He smiled and repeated, "Good girl, Roxie!"

Then he walked across the soft green ground, turned to me and said, "Come, Roxie. Come!"

Say what?

A squirrel caught my eye as it ran up a tree. I stumbled toward it. Out of reach, it looked backed, twitched its tail, and mocked me.

"Roxie, come here!" I saw Steve on his knees waving at me.

Ok, 'Roxie Come.' Is that my name?

Steve came to me, scooped me up in his arms, and entered the building.

"This is your new home, Roxie."

The first thing I notice were little platforms from the bottom where he placed me. And these platforms rose as far as I could see. He walked up to the top, turned around, and said, "Come, Roxie! Come up the stairs!"

Are you kidding me?

I sniffed at the first stair, backed up, and lay down with my head between my paws. I looked up at Steve.

"Come Roxie! Come!"

Ain't happening.

He came down to me, and up we went, me in his arm.

He set me down, and again I saw another collection of these little platforms in front of me.

We went through the same process as before with Steve going ahead and calling to me, me not moving, Steve returning and carrying me up.

Finally, at the top of this last series of platforms, I was placed on a floor in a big bright room. There were lots of objects in the room much bigger than me. Some seemed soft. Others hard. What caught my attention was a big wire box in front of me. It was huge! About the size of 4 of those puppy crates at the building where I was groggy.

"Here you go, Roxie," Steve said as he gently placed me inside the crate. There was a lot of soft stuff on the bottom of the crate. It felt nice. The door was open. Two bowls sat just inside the door but off the soft stuff. I moved toward them and sniffed. I nibbled from one and lapped up water from the other. I nibbled some more and then explored the crate. It was the biggest box I had ever been in. And it was quiet.

Steve and Hoppi smiled. Hoppi said, "I think she likes it. Let's leave the door open so she can go in and out on her own." I seemed to please them.

I stepped out of the crate a few paces and squatted.

"No!" Steve yelled. He pulled me up, holding me at arm's distance. Hoppi opened a door, and out we stepped, down another long series of those little platforms.

How many of these things are in this place?

We were back in the soft green area where I was a few minutes earlier. Steve placed me on the ground.

Thanks, but I lost the urge from all that commotion.

But a few minutes later, I squatted and peed.

"Good girl, Roxie! Good girl!" Steve scratched my ears and gave me a little piece of food, saying, "Biscuit."

I thought my name was Roxie.

I ate the piece of food. It tasted good. Yum!

Again, Steve tried to get me to follow him up a few stairs. I was not having it. At. All.

"Roxie, here ya go. One stair at a time." And, with that he'd place me on the first one.

Nice of him to pick me up and place me down, but I'm still not budging.

He lifted and carried me the rest of the way, stroking my head. When we got back inside, I spied my crate, entered it, and ate some more. Then I curled up in the corner of the crate and closed my eyes. It had been an eventful day. I drifted off to sleep, content in the quiet.

Beyond the Biscuit

For me, the first time I saw stairs, they seemed impossible. They scared me, and I did not move. Has that ever happened to you? When was there an obstacle in your life that seemed insurmountable? How did you finally move up and forward? Who helped you? What did you learn?

COMFORT ZONES

HOW DO YOU STRETCH YOUR COMFORT ZONES TO TAKE ON NEW AND, MAYBE, SCARY CHALLENGES?

I settled into my new home with Hoppi and Steve.
I had two crates, one upstairs and one down in the bedroom. I heard Steve call them "puppy condos." I also had a fluff pillow beside Steve's desk in his office. I've heard over the years that some dogs don't take to crates well. They bark, claw, howl, and some even bloody themselves to get out.

I don't get that.

I gladly went in and out of my crates on my own during the day. At night, when Steve would close the gate, I curled up and slept. I think, maybe, it was because Steve and Hoppi always spoke so highly of me as I entered either area. For instance, if I had peed in the house or dropped some pooh in front of the sink, no one ever said, "Bad dog! Go to your crate now. Bad dog!"

And after the first few days, there was no need for Steve to place a bowl of food or water in the crate to lure me in. I walked in gladly. The crate was always associated with my toys and "Good, Roxie" or "Good night, Roxie. Good dog" or "Here's a biscuit!"

By the way, I quickly learned about "biscuit." I still will do most anything to get a little biscuit. Steve calls me a "biscuit tart." I think that is a good thing.

In any event, me and my crates were as one. As I became more accustomed to my new home, I retreated often to my puppy condos and fluff pillows. For me, they offered security, peace, and solace. They became my comfort zones.

Within these zones, I could catch my breath and rest. Then, rested and calm, I'd venture out to explore another area or to check on the whereabouts of Steve. Each outing helped me gain more confidence. I could feel a bounce in my paws as I scouted the area.

I kind of remember back in the puppy room that some puppies curled up, as if to hide, in the back of their crates. Cowering. Others would stand at the crate door and whimper to be released. Me, I took the time to think about where I'd been on my latest excursion. No matter where I'd been, crate time became my quiet and alone time.

When I had rested enough, I always looked forward to walking out of the crate. With each exploration, I became more confident about my safety. I grew with each opportunity. I stretched my legs and my comfort zone with each new encounter.

At times I was scared. Like those stairs that never seemed to end. But if I did not learn to walk up and down those little wooden platforms, I would have missed all the yard had to offer.

Steve was patient, though I could tell he got impatient at times with my slow and methodical way of navigating the steps. He would help by carrying me down a step, place me on it, walk ahead of me, and then encourage me to follow. At first, he'd place a biscuit on the next few steps in front of me. He was smart! A strategically placed biscuit always motivated me forward.

Comfort zones, like my crates, provide shelter and reflection opportunities. A place to retreat from the stresses of the world. Comfort zones can become a crutch, though. I would have missed so much if I had not learned to risk and be vulnerable.

I heard Steve say to Hoppi that we find life beyond our comfort zones.

Yes. We. Do.

But one day, my comfort zone expanded far beyond my puppy condos.

Beyond the Biscuit

Where are your comfort zones? How and when do you use them? How do you stretch your comfort zones to take on new and, maybe, scary challenges? How do these challenges help you grow?

THE LITTLE YELLOW BUILDING

CONSIDER A SAFE PLACE THAT MAKES YOU FEEL ALIVE AND FREE. HOW DOES IT ALLOW YOU TO CHALLENGE YOUR COMFORT ZONES AND GROW?

I love where I live, whom I live with, and what I get to do each day. I have soft indoor areas to rest, sunny and shady outside spaces to stretch and explore, and yummy food to eat. And biscuits. Just love to hear *anyone* say, "Biscuit!" I am never too tired to get up when I hear that word.

A word, if I may, about biscuits. I'd eat a whole box if I could. Steve knows that and only gives me a little bit at a time. And I mean *a little bit.* The biscuits are very tiny and, although he thinks I do not notice, he breaks the small biscuits into even smaller bites.

Steve and I spend a lot of time together at home. He doesn't leave the house in his car like I notice the neighbors do each morning. I hear he and Hoppi talk about people going to *work* to earn money to buy food. I'm guessing he doesn't earn much, so that is why the biscuits are so small. That's ok. I'm willing to help with the budget by eating smaller biscuits. That's just how I roll. Anything for my person.

At times Steve does take me to play with other dogs. At first, I was a bit hesitant. You know, kind of out of my comfort zone. It took patience for him and me to feel at ease with other dogs around.

My all-time favorite place to visit is the little yellow building that is only a short car ride from our home. When our car stops in front of the little yellow building, I get excited. It is the only time I catch myself yelping and fidgeting on the backseat.

On the other side of the yellow building's front door is where I get quality time with my canine buds. When I first visited, I had never seen as many running around in one place. We have the biggest yard to run and jump and, well, just be dogs. Love it!

Karen, Erin, and their human friends make us feel so good. They play with us, and they make sure none of us gets rough. Sometimes they have special humans come visit us. I think they are humans, but they dress kind of funny. Nothing like anything I see our neighbors wear. One comes when the days are colder. He dresses in red. And has a white beard. We sit next to him and Erin takes a photo. Not sure why. But since my pup friends sit, I do, too.

Every so often, Erin brings me a special treat. It looks like a huge bone—biggest I've ever seen. But it is soft, not hard like a biscuit. It tastes like pumpkin and peanut butter. And there is usually something on it like a "1." Most recently, there was a "4" on one of these fluffy-taste-so-good-gooey-colorful bones.

When I get these bones, Erin puts a hat on my head or drapes something around my neck. She seems to like it and smiles. I sit there knowing soon I have a big treat ahead of me. Yum, yum, and yum!

At times, I won't see Steve and Hoppi for a few days. I play all day with my pup friends and then dream all night in my own crate inside the little yellow building. The next day, we are all out in the big yard again.

I love the little yellow building and the people and pups inside it. I feel safe, alive, and free.

Beyond the Biscuit

Consider a safe place that makes you feel alive and free. Where is that place for you? What makes it feel safe? How does it allow you to challenge your comfort zones and grow?

TWERKING SQUIRRELS!

IS IT POSSIBLE WE MIGHT JUMP TO INCORRECT CONCLUSIONS?

I had settled into my new home quite nicely. Steve and I had developed a morning routine of going to the backyard, where he would follow me until I squatted.

"Good girl, Roxie!" Then I got a biscuit. Not a bad exchange.

The backyard was mine to explore. Untethered, I could run, sniff, roll, or just lay and ponder nature. Truth be told, I love to ponder. More quiet time when I could look up at the giant trees above me. Birds fluttered. And then, of course, there were the squirrels.

Those squirrels!

They would come down the tree trunk, tails twerking every which way. Stopping and starting. I'd watch, quietly rise to my paws, and stealthily move toward them. Not sure what I would do if I ever caught one. Just wanted them to know that I was top dog, and this was my domain. Then it would happen.

With a jump, the squirrel would be off the tree to the top of the fence and then scurry the length of the yard. That was my cue to go—and off I would run toward the fence. The squirrel above me and moving quickly until it reached the other end and up another tree.

I'd stop and look up at it.

Guess you know who rules here. I'm Roxie. Nice to meet you.

Dumb twerking invader would just look at me, making stupid sounds. Mocking me.

I would turn and kick dirt.

Beyond the Biscuit

Over time, I have learned to co-exist with the squirrels. I still don't get what they do or how they do it—but I have learned they are not there to bother me. Think of the last time you were challenged by someone you did not understand. How did you handle it? What did you learn? Is it possible we might jump to conclusions that are incorrect?

PUPPY OBEDIENCE

WAS STEVE LEAVING ME? I DIDN'T UNDERSTAND THIS.

One morning, after the yard and my breakfast, Steve loaded me into the car. Sitting in the backseat, I watched the world go by. So much to see!

When we finally got out of the car, we walked into the biggest room I had ever seen. And scents! Oh my! I smelled dogs, cats, birds, rodents, food, biscuits (Yum!), and more. More scents than the puppy room and my backyard combined. So much to take in that I was panting as if I had just run after a pack of squirrels.

Steve talked with a man named Bill who walked us to a small area that had a little fence around it in the front corner of the big room. Another dog sat unceremoniously in the fenced area. He was kind of squat, fat, and jowly. Panted a lot with slobber coming from the side of his mouth. Not a whole lot of oomph, if you know what I mean. I forget his name. And, the not-impressive dog had a young woman with him. She paid more attention to a thin thing she held in her hand and kept swiping her finger across.

For the next eight weeks, Steve and I would enter this room and play with Bill. Though, I must admit, after a while it began to feel like work. Lots of commands to do this and that. I noticed that

Steve began to carry biscuits in his pocket every time we left the house. And I started hearing the same words again and again.

Sit. Stay. Down. Come. Wait. Leave it! Watch me. OK!

Didn't make much sense to me. Steve would say one of those words and I would just look at him, my head tilted to one side.

What in the world are you talking about?

"Sit, Roxie, sit."

Huh?

"Sit, Roxie, sit." And then he would gently place his hand on my butt and guide it to the floor. I got a biscuit and smiles from Steve.

Ok. I like this.

I quickly figured out if I did what Steve said, I'd get "biscuited."

One day we walked around the big room. I was on a leash, Steve by my side. We passed other dogs who came into the big room with their people. We passed bags piled as high as our backyard fence, and each one smelled of delightful food and treats. Down every isle more and more bags of aroma. I pulled at the leash, so I could get closer and sniff the bags. I wanted to linger.

"Leave it, Roxie, leave it." And, we kept walking until we returned to Bill at the fenced area. He was smiling.

"Good dog, Roxie! Sit."

I wagged my tail. Bill scratched my ears. And, I got a biscuit. I liked this game.

One day, Bill hooked me to the longest leash I'd ever seen. It looked like it could have stretched across my backyard at home.

Steve took the rope and stood beside me. I sat. He patted my head. I looked up at him.

What, no biscuit?

I came to learn that I didn't know when I would get a treat. Hmm.

"Stay, Roxie, stay." He walked away from me. I got up to follow.

"Sit, Roxie, sit. Good girl. Stay."

I assumed the position. He walked to the end of the rope, turned, and looked at me.

"Come, Roxie, come!" he said waving his arms and being all excited.

I took off and ran to him.

"Good girl, Roxie. Sit."

Biscuit! (Yum!)

The last day we played with Bill in the big room, I had to do the hardest thing yet.

We walked out of the little fenced area into one of the paths by the wall. I remember my nose up in the air taking in all the smells. Bill was waiting for Steve and me.

"Sit, Roxie, sit. Stay!" Steve said as he walked in front of me like he had done before.

Hey, you forgot to hold the leash!

He walked and walked and walked. Never looked back. When he got to the far end of the building, he did something I could not believe. It scared me a little. He turned to the right and was gone!

Where did he go? I don't see him anymore.

Bill stood off to the side of me and watched, but he did nothing to find Steve.

I just sat there, like Steve told me to do. But I tell you, I did not like it. It felt like the night in the box when that person left me on the side of the road. Was Steve leaving me, too? I didn't understand this. My heart beat a little faster.

So, there I sat, intently staring to where I saw him turn out of my sight. No Steve. Then I heard him, but he was coming at me from the other direction. He had walked around the entire big room and was walking back to me.

He didn't leave me!
I started to move until I heard, "Stay, Roxie, stay."
Steve got closer. He stopped a few paces in front of me and looked at me.
"Come, Roxie, come!"
I ran to him and nose nuzzled him, excited as I could be. I got a biscuit and more importantly, I still had Steve.
"Good, girl, Roxie. You stayed! Good girl."
Little did I know; I would soon be staying by myself for a lot longer than it would take Steve to walk around that big room.

Beyond the Biscuit

Think of the last time you were challenged to learn a new set of skills. What were they, and why did you need them? Who helped you develop the new skills, and how did they help you grow as a person?

WATER FELL FROM THEIR EYES

HOW DID YOU NAVIGATE THROUGH A MAJOR LIFE CHALLENGE? WHO HELPED? WHAT LESSONS DID YOU LEARN?

Humans have this habit of shedding water from their eyes. Mostly when they are sad or hurting.

I had settled into my new life with Steve and Hoppi. Each day, I'd explore the backyard, prance around with my toys in the house, and walk with Steve. And each day, we'd walk a little further than the day before. First, we walked to the end of the path where the cars were parked. Then we made it to the big green area across from our house where we found lots of grass, dirt, water, and scents. There were scents everywhere! Dogs, cats, raccoons, coyotes, ducks, and more. I moved to the left, to the right, and straight ahead with my nose barely off the dirt. Sniff, sniff, sniff.

And, each day we'd venture a little further before I got tired and would just lay down, Steve would give a little tug on the leash to urge me forward. I was done. So, we'd turn and head back to our house and my comfort zones.

"We'll make it to the beach next week, Roxie. Beach! You'll love the beach."

Steve always smiled when he said "beach." So, I'd wag my tail. Maybe "beach" is like "biscuit," I thought.

Hoppi left the house each day for what I heard them refer to as *work*. She wore a uniform, and she always looked so good. I was glad she was part of our home.

When Hoppi left, I stayed with Steve, which was good. I'd follow him from room to room. Sometimes, I'd sleep. Well, ok, most times I slept. Life was good.

Then water started coming from their eyes.

I could sense that Hoppi was sad, and so was Steve.

"The biopsy shows cancer," she said. I looked at each of them, and I could tell they were not happy. The water ran down their cheeks, and I did not understand any of the words. They said *cancer* a lot. They hugged, and eventually the water stopped.

Life changed for me at that moment. Oh, Steve and Hoppi still loved on me. My walks took us a little further each day. Just like Steve promised, we made it to the beach. And I loved it. I, also, spent more time alone in the house.

"Hoppi and I have to go see the doctor, Roxie. Here's a biscuit. I'll be back soon."

I would go into my crate with expectations of "yum, yum, yum" circling in my head. He would drop a biscuit on the floor and gently close the gate. I'd nibble, curl up, listen to the music that came from a little box outside my puppy condo, and dream of our next walk.

This went on for longer than I had been with Steve and Hoppi. They would leave. Steve would come back and let me in the backyard, love on me, and sometimes take me for a walk around the big scented area across from our house. And, then, back in the crate, and he would leave again.

I would sleep and dream of the scents, the beach, and the biscuits. Mostly the biscuits. At some point, I'd be awakened by the door opening. I'd hear Steve and Hoppi. I remember that Hoppi would lay her head down on the bed and sleep. She looked tired. Steve and I would go for a walk while Hoppi would rest.

This became our new routine. I did not mind it. I had my comfort zone to curl up in. And, there were the biscuits. Not many, but always the promise of one. I had Steve and Hoppi. The days were getting cooler.

And, then I got sick.

Beyond the Biscuit

Sometimes, when life seems to be going along just fine, *it* happens. You know what I mean. Something occurs that seems to challenge life as you know it. Some people fall apart. Some grow stronger. Think of such a time in your life. How did you navigate through that major life challenge? Who helped? What lessons did you learn?

ONE DAY IT ALL CHANGED

THINK OF A TIME WHEN A CHALLENGE LED YOU TO RENEWED PURPOSE. HOW DID YOU CHANGE?

I remember when we finally made it to the beach early one morning. I sensed it before we got there. With my nose in the air I could smell scents I never detected in the park near our home. And I heard a noise. A roar!

It sounded like when Steve poured water in my bowl, only louder. Like all the bowls in the puppy room and more. Much more.

I stopped when my paws first hit the soft, cool sand. I kind of slid in it. Then I pulled the leash and jumped with excitement. Steve laughed.

"You're a wack-a-doodle!"

The beach became our daily routine. We'd get there in time to see the orange ball pop out of the water. Steve always remained still as he gazed toward the water.

"It's a new sun and new opportunities, Roxie."

I met new friends, like Maker's. He was much bigger than me and red with longer hair and a narrow snout. I had to sit as Maker's got closer.

"Watch me, Roxie."

But I'd watch Maker's and tug at the leash. Maker's would sniff me and turn his back. I learned that he was the top dog. And, I think, an older dog. He did not have the energy I did. That was ok. I liked his smell. At times, we'd lie down in the sand and roll around. That was a lot of fun. I felt like I was his best bud.

I met small dogs like Coco and Gigi. Big ones like Bear and Cotton. We were all becoming friends. And there was Baby. I liked her best. We would always jump and play when we'd meet. Steve would give us each a biscuit.

Then one day it all changed.

We had just come back from the beach.

"Look at Roxie's mouth," Steve said as he held me for Hoppi to see. "It looks like fleshy cauliflower. And there are smaller ones on her gums." He pulled my lips up to show.

We went for a car ride to a building he had taken me to a few days after I had left the puppy room. I remember a kindly and tall man with white hair, Dr. Moody, pushing and prodding all over my body. He even put a slender stick up my pooh hole.

Hey!

And I still remembered the needles. But he gave me a biscuit, so all was good!

This time we saw a nice woman who placed me on a table.

"Papilloma Virus. Like warts on Roxie's gums." She said matter-of-factly. "Not much to do but let it run its course. Not unusual for a puppy. They could get it from other dogs. You should keep her away from other animals, though, until they go away."

So, now whenever I would see Baby we could not touch. Same with Maker's and the other dogs. I could not go to the little yellow building to play or stay overnight.

I missed my friends.

I could tell Steve was worried. He would check me daily. He wanted those things in my mouth to go away, too. You see this was still the time

Hoppi was not feeling well, either. They would go away during the day. Steve seemed a bit stressed. I was glad to be near him. He needed me.

As the days went by, I roamed the house when they left for short periods of time. First, he would take me for a walk to pee and pooh.

"OK, Roxie, we trust you to guard the house. Don't be a wack-a-doodle."

He'd then smile and toss me a few biscuits. Yum! And he would turn on soft music for me. I'd eat the biscuits, sniff around the house, and then curl up for a nice nap.

Steve brought me to see the nice lady at Dr. Moody's building every so often. She would pull at my mouth and shake her head. That meant there would be more alone time. No problem. Steve was always with me. His presence helped me get through this dreadfully boring time.

When the days became a lot colder, and the sun was not out as long, we finally got good news.

"She's good!" I heard the nice lady say. "She can play with other pups again."

Steve brought me to the little yellow building to play for the day. I was happy! Steve and Hoppi were relieved.

We had once again been there for each other.

Beyond the Biscuit

In the last story, something happened to Hoppi that influenced Steve and me. In this story, when I developed the warts, that had an impact on Steve and Hoppi. In both stories, with the support of one another, we made it through difficult times. In each challenging moment, each person's purpose changed. Think of a time when a challenge led you to renewed purpose. How did you change? Who was there for you? When have you had to be there for someone else?

ANOTHER TEST

HOW OFTEN DO YOU TREAT YOURSELF AND OTHER BEINGS WITH DIGNITY AND RESPECT?

As I approached my third year with Steve and Hoppi, I reflected one day while stretched out in the back yard watching another one of those pesky twerking squirrels dance across the fence top. They *are* obnoxious.

Steve and I had navigated puppy obedience class.

Check!

We got through the fleshy cauliflower that had grown all over my lips and mouth.

Check!

I played regularly at the little yellow building.

Check!

Hoppi was healthy.

Check!

Steve and I spent quality time together each day.

Check!

I had an office fluff pillow.

Check!

Sunrise walks on the beach, afternoon romps in the park, and biscuits!

Check! Check! Check!

At times I was a bit bored, but that's a dog's life. I learned to deal with it. But Steve would surprise me every so often. Such as one late afternoon when we hopped into the car and drove toward town.

"Roxie," he said as we drove over the bridge. "Tonight, we start Canine Good Citizen Class. The nice lady will train us so we can become a pet therapy team."

I tilted my head from the back seat and looked toward him. Other than my name, nothing else made sense. So, I looked at the water flowing beneath us. Whatever and wherever we go, I trust Steve.

"Eventually, we will be able to visit people in hospitals, schools, and other places. People won't much care about me, but they will be excited to see you. You and I have a lot of work to do. I know you can do it. And, of course, there will be biscuits in it for you, too."

Biscuits! He got my attention. Feed me and I will come.

Well, for several weeks, we traveled across the bridge to a big lot without cars. There were other dogs. Mostly what people call *Doodle dogs*. I did not look like them. We couldn't play like I did with my pup friends. This was all business.

Each night we would watch one dog do something, and then Steve and I would do it. Sometimes the nice lady up front, Stacy, made us do it three or four times. We both had to really concentrate.

On what ended up being the last night, we went to the big lot without cars. As Steve, me, and the other dogs and humans waited in the big lot, there was a lot of commotion. I thought it was kind of odd, but I played along. For instance, one person came by banging a pot and pan. Another person, Mel, pushed a chair with wheels under it.

There was one dog that sat there, and Steve and I had to pass by. What did I do? What any self-respecting dog would do! I crossed in front of Steve to initiate the doggie handshake. Heck, I'm a polite, friendly, and respectful canine.

Unfortunately, Stacy did not like that, and we had to begin again. I started hearing Steve utter, "Leave it, Roxie. Leave it!" A lot.

At the end of all the different things Stacy made us do, she thought she would play with my mind. Steve gave the leash to another person and then walked away from me. He never looked back. He walked a good piece down the big lot without cars and disappeared from my sight. People looked at me. I sat there. Heck, they did not know what happened in that big box store with all the aromas when Steve left me for what seemed like longer than I had been alive at that time.

So, I sat.

Finally, Stacy said something, and I saw Steve come back toward me. Like I knew he would, thank you!

By the end of that night, Steve got some paper and I posed for a photo with a ribbon. Not sure what all that was about but, I do know that Steve and I got a little bit closer and knew each other better as a result of these trips over the bridge to work with the nice lady in the big lot without cars.

Everybody hugged on that last night. I saw the smile on Steve's face, and I was happy.

As I dozed off to sleep later that night, I remembered Steve talking to Hoppi about what he and I had done in the big lot without cars. The program helped dogs and their people work well together and respect each other as well as the other beings in the big lot with no cars. For instance:

- Steve had to sign a pledge to take care of my "health needs, safety, exercise, training and quality of life." *He does.*
- I had to remain calm and polite when approached by a *friendly stranger.* I was not to jump or growl at the person. *And, I did not!*
- I also had to be of healthy weight, properly groomed, and alert. Steve was reminded to praise and encourage me. *I am, he did, and he does.*
- We walked through a bunch of people to test my ability to remain focused and not to show resentment for those around me. *That was easy. I do not resent anyone or anything. Well, maybe those dreaded twerking squirrels. They mock me!*
- They tested my ability to handle noise and other distractions. *No problem!*

Wow. Caring for health needs and quality of life. Remaining calm, not jumping on, or showing resentment toward another being. Practice and apply strategies to remain focused on the present and not be distracted by environmental noise.

I thought, if all human beings treated each other with the same dignity as expected of us dogs and their people, what a wonderful world it must be.

Beyond the Biscuit

How well do you:

- Care for your health and quality of life?
- Add to the quality of life for others?
- Resist distractions from environmental noise?
- Treat yourself and others with dignity and respect?

MORE WHEELS, PRACTICE, AND SMILES

WHAT KEEPS YOU MOVING BEYOND THE BISCUIT?

Steve knows and hangs with nice humans. I first met Marcie at an outside table between two buildings. It was a cool morning as we walked up to where she was sitting.

"Sit, Roxie, sit."

Marcie smiled at me. She and Steve talked about *evaluations*. I was hoping for a biscuit.

We then showed Marcie what we could do as a team. Walking. Stopping. Sitting. Turning. Staying. We looked smart!

Steve and Marcie talked some more. They smiled, said goodbye, and then we left.

A few days later we met Marcie at another building I had never seen before. The three of us walked into a large room. Very large. Bigger than the one where Steve left me that time with Bill.

As we walked on the cool floor, we passed more wheels than I had ever seen or heard at one time. I saw wheels on big baskets that people pushed. Other wheels were on long platforms with pieces of wood on them. Those wheels rumbled and rattled a lot. Very loud.

"Watch me, Roxie." Steve walked us closer to the wheels.

While the wheels were obnoxious, I tuned them out and listened to Steve.

We both followed Marcie as we turned left, then right, then left, and left, and so on. We walked from one end of the building to the other. Then we walked to the back of the building in and out of aisles with shelves stacked, it seemed, almost to the ceiling. At one point, we stopped. Marcie and Steve sat, and I rested on the floor. I quietly watched the noisy wheels go by. I heard Marcie say that I had done well.

Of course.

The next time we met Marcie, we entered a much smaller building. The wheels here were quieter. Some had chairs on them with people being pushed through narrow hallways. Some wheels had beds on top of them, with people sleeping in the beds. I think they were sleeping as their eyes were closed from what I could see.

Again, I followed Steve's commands as Marcie led us from one room to another. We stopped and talked with some of the people who were in smaller rooms with beds on wheels.

Later, as we walked back to our car, Marcie waived goodbye with a smile.

"Good job, Roxie. Good job," Steve said as I jumped into the back seat. "You didn't bark or get spooked. We are getting closer."

Closer to *what* I didn't know. But Steve was happy, so I felt good. Listening to the music coming from the front of the car, I slept all the way home.

We did a few more visits with Marcie. One day we went to a person who poked, pushed, and pulled on me. He listened to my heart. He smiled. I heard him say I was healthy. Marcie smiled again.

A few days later, Steve hugged me, rubbed my neck and whispered in my ear.

"We can do pet therapy now at the hospital, Roxie. You did well. Thank you!"

He gave me a biscuit.

Yum!

And yet, there would be a demon I had to confront—within and without.

Beyond the Biscuit

I have learned during my time with Steve that to do things well in life requires effort. Like mornings on the beach. While we love our sunrises on the sand, we must walk to the ocean, walk along the water's edge, and then walk home. At times, I get tired, but the effort is worth it. The same with working with Marcie, Stacy, and Bill. They required a lot of concentration and practice for Steve and me. And it was worth it when we finished what they wanted us to do.

Can you remember a time when you had to go through a lot of training and practice to get something important? Maybe you got rewarded every so often, like when I get a biscuit. What kept you going besides the reward? What kept you moving beyond the biscuit? How did you feel when you finally finished? What lessons did you learn?

PEOPLE ON TOP OF THE BOARDS ON TOP OF THE WHEELS

DO YOU LIKE HOW FEAR MAKES YOU FEEL AND BEHAVE?

Steve and I settled into a comfortable routine. When we'd walk to the garage, I'd patiently wait for him to slip on his sneakers or sandals and place a few biscuits into his left pocket. It was always the same pocket. He knew I would like to snack on one or two during our walk.

All the while I lay on the floor, head between my extended front legs, and my eyes following him around as he got ready.

The last thing he'd do is reach for my leash and stand over me. Without a word from him, I would rise and sit. *Snap* went the lead, and off we'd go out the door, down the walk, through the gate, and ready for our adventure.

"Good girl, Roxie. You're such a good girl."

He was pleased. He was happy. All was good.

Until.

Until I'd hear *that* noise. Not sure why it bothered me so. Well, it did more than *bother* me. It sent me into an *out-of-body experience*. I became another dog. Or so it felt.

I often heard *it* before Steve. I could feel myself tense up before I ever saw the noisemaker. Early on, this caught Steve by surprise. We'd be walking, leash loose in his hand, and then, suddenly, something would come over me.

I'd hear the scraping of those small wheels along the street. At first it was faint and then increasingly louder as it got closer to us. Then I'd see the human standing on top of the board on top of the wheels, weaving back and forth as he rumbled down the street.

The first time I almost pulled Steve to the ground as I went for the wheels whizzing by me.

"Bad dog! No!"

But I could not help myself. I was focused on those blasted wheels.

I never went after the person on top of the board on top of the wheels. But I was bothered such that my muscles tightened, I growled, barked, and panted. I did not even recognize my own self at these moments.

Eventually, Steve became as good as me sensing when the people on top of the boards on top of the wheels were coming. In fact, at times, he'd know it before I did. Not sure how he pulled that off. He *is* good!

I'd feel the leash shorten, and he would straddle my body, holding me by the leash with one hand, while his other hand cradled my chest.

"Roxie, leave it! Good girl."

As I turned and saw those menacing wheels approaching, I could feel my gut moving to my throat and get caught in my mouth.

"*Grrrrr!*"

"No, Roxie. Leave it. Leave it."

Quickly the person on top of the board on top of the wheels would pass. I'd intently follow it with my eyes. As soon as it was beyond, Steve would begin to loosen his hold.

"Good, Roxie!" And I got a biscuit. Yum!

While I was still a jumble of mixed emotions, Steve's touch—and the biscuit—helped.

At times, Steve brings me to a park that has what looks like a huge hard bowl in the middle. Kind of like a small street that goes around in a tight and tilted circle. As we get closer, I hear them and then see them. A lot of young people on top of the boards on top of the wheels. More than I have ever seen at any one time in one place. Up, down, and around they whirl in the tight and tilted circle. Loud noise.

Why is he doing this? This is killing me!

Where one person on top of the board on top of the wheels got me all tense, now I'll see five or six at one time. Dreadful, I tell you. Dreadful.

We sit on a bench outside the tilted tight hard circle. Steve holds me close and whispers, "Good Roxie. It's ok." And he gives me a biscuit.

I learned quickly if I want a biscuit, I better not growl. So, quietly I ate my biscuit. And I give the people on top of the boards on top of the wheels a squinty look of disapproval.

"*Come on dudes, get a life!*"

I'm not sure why I do not like those wheels. After all, other wheels never bother me. Whenever we visit people who are in beds or chairs on wheels, or who pull bags on wheels, it never phases me.

The biscuits helped. I got less angry and less scared as they went by. But I still did not like those people on top of the boards on top of the wheels. Nothing against them. I just did not appreciate their mode of transportation. Much prefer the quiet of Steve's car.

Then, I learned that humans had other strange habits than rolling around on top of the boards on top of the wheels.

_____

Beyond the Biscuit

I admit it, these people on top of the boards on top of the wheels scare me. Partly because of the noise. Partly because I don't understand them. I don't like how I feel around them. Steve is helping me learn to fear less and co-exist. What do you fear? How do you react to this thing, person, place, or issue? Do you like how fear makes you feel and behave? What have you done to learn to co-exist with someone or something that creates an uneasy feeling for you?

EAR BUTTS

I'M JUST A DOG. WHAT DO I KNOW?

Humans have always been nice to me. Even the one who left me in a box a long time ago did the best he or she could. All of Steve's friends always make me wag my tail. They call my name, scratch my head, and pat me on my haunches. Nice! Some even have a biscuit for me. I know who they are as I've come to know their scents. I could recognize them with my eyes closed.

Every so often, though, I smell an odd odor on some people. It comes from a stick in their hands. They put it to their mouths, create fire at the end of the stick, and then blow out smoke. It stinks. I've seen Steve turn up his nose at my pooh, but it is nowhere near as foul as that smoke.

Yes, that is correct. My pooh does not stink.

Some of these smoke breathers will drop their small fire sticks on the ground, step on them and walk away. When Steve finds one, he will pick it up, put it in a bag, and throw it away. I've heard Steve complain often about *butts* on the beach and how they can harm the animals in the water. It bothers him and I think he must have talked to some of these people about their nasty habit. At least, I think he has from what I've been observing lately. I am intrigued by the odd new behavior of the fire-stick-smoke-breathers-who-drop-their-butts-on-the-beach.

Rather than drop the butts on the sand, some humans now seem to place them in their ears! I know. I know. That sounds very strange. Even to a dog. But I cross my chest with my paw. And that is not the only odd thing I notice when I see this strange behavior.

You see, they always have one butt hanging from each ear. Yep—a total of two ear butts. And Steve thinks I'm a wack-a-doodle!

If someone stops to talk to them, they are polite. They usually will remove their ear butts, speak, and smile. As they walk away, they reinsert the ear butts in each ear. And there they dangle. I guess they are happy that they have not littered the ground. I can see them singing and dancing. Strange.

But, again, what do I know. I am just glad they carry the ear butts away with a smile and a song.

Humans. Nice, but they have strange habits.

Beyond the Biscuit

We all have habits. Some, like exercise, help us lead a healthy life. Others, unfortunately, can be harmful to us, those around us, and our planet. They may even distract us from our purpose in life. What habit of yours has helped you lead a life of meaning and growth? Which habit has created complications for your life?

COUCH TIME

WHERE IS YOUR GO-TO PLACE FOR RETREAT?

I am a lucky dog. Each day brings me sunrise beach walks, good food, comfortable beds, and loving humans. Oh, and biscuits, of course.

I, also, like that I have my space, and Steve and Hoppi have theirs. They respect my crates and fluff pillows. Not once have they attempted to squeeze into my crates and cozy up to me. It's my space for my alone time. I appreciate the respect.

And, I do not get into their crates or fluff pillows as often as I would like. As big as their spaces are, you think there would be room for me. One of Steve's crates has arms and folds backwards, allowing him to kick his feet up on a little platform. He sometimes will lay stretched out and still. Every so often, a snort will come from him. And then quiet. He doesn't stay long; about the time it takes us to walk to the beach and back. He calls these little timeouts *power naps*.

Sometimes, if I sit beside him, place my head on his leg and look into his eyes, he will say, "OK!" and tap his leg. That is my cue to jump up, curl at the end of his crate, in between his legs and power nap with him. Nice!

One night, Hoppi laid out a blanket on one of the long crates they have in the TV room. They call it a *couch*. She and Steve sat on either end, and they called to me. I had already eaten. I hadn't peed in the house. I know I had not chewed anything. Other than a few toys they placed in my crates, I never chew on people things. Chewing seems like a waste of time. I could just as easily use that time to power nap.

Well, I walked over to the couch, head lowered, not knowing what to expect.

"Sit."

Steve looked at me for a few moments.

"OK!" He said as he patted the top of the couch. I jumped up and landed on the softest fluff pillow I'd ever experienced. I froze, not knowing what to do. Steve and Hoppi had left a space between them about the size of my belly. I turned, turned, and turned again. I curled between them, my head coming to rest on Steve's lap. He stroked my head.

Harrumph! I sighed and drifted off to sleep.

This became a nightly event. After they finished eating their food, one of them would spread out the blanket. Soon I was up between them.

Hoppi started doing the same thing in the morning with me. When Steve and I return from our beach walk, she is sitting on the couch, blanket stretched out. She holds a cup with steam coming from it. And she has a big square thing in her lap, moving her hand up, down and right. I noticed that a light and colors come from the square. Sometimes I hear a human speak or music play. One time I saw dogs flash across the square. Hoppi laughed. I don't get it.

But what I do get is quality couch time with Hoppi and Steve each day.

Beyond the Biscuit

Where is your go-to place for retreat? How does this time help you relax, grow, and reaffirm your purpose?

47

READING THE PAPER

HOW DO YOU STAY FOCUSED ON WHAT OR WHO IS IN FRONT OF YOU?

On our morning walks to the sand and water, I quickly noticed something different about how Steve and I walk. Over time, I have trained him to walk more like me, but it is an ongoing challenge for him.

You see, he walks with his head up. He either looks straight ahead of him or up into the sky. Especially on the beach. I've noticed he looks out over the water and seems utterly lost as the sun pops up. He snaps photos. And he talks with other humans about the colors and textures.

I guess that's all good. It makes Steve smile. I am glad for him.

Me, I'd rather look toward the ground. In fact, I don't just cast my eyes to the ground, I put my nose to the ground. There is so much that humans miss by pointing their noses to the sky. That's probably why Steve walks so fast, and I must slow him down with a little tug on the leash.

"There you go, Roxie," he says with a smile and a tad of impatience, "always reading the paper."

Whatever.

I want to know who has been where I am—and how they feel.

My sniffer can tell me if another animal has recently been at the tree I am passing. I smell and, at times, lick the dog pee.

"Roxie, no. Yuck!"

Steve, and I think most humans, just don't get it. The scents and tastes tell me a lot. Like if a friend is nearby. I can even sense if the animal was in some sort of stress or if I should be on alert. Of course, if there is danger, I am there to warn Steve. Think of these as breaking news alerts.

Have you ever noticed how dogs will sometimes walk right up to a spot that another dog peed on, and then smell and pee on top of that spot? Sometimes we do that to show we are with that dog—a friend of ours. Other times, we want to make sure others know we have been there. What I really like doing is peeing and then walking a few steps, stopping, and then kicking up a lot of dirt. Makes me feel good, and it spreads my scent a little further. I want others to know I've been around.

Steve misses so much. I feel it's my job to search the area for signs of danger. It's the least I can do for him as he keeps looking up.

I'll read the paper and let him know with a tug on the leash if something needs his attention.

Beyond the Biscuit

How do you stay focused on and curious about what or who is in front of you? Do you look people in the eyes and speak to them? Or are you distracted? How can the environment give you clues?

HELPING STEVE

WHAT HAVE YOU DONE TO HELP ANOTHER BEING GET THROUGH A DIFFICULT TIME?

"Are you kidding me?"

I heard Steve speak, but only I was in the room. That was not unusual as he often speaks words to himself. I had gotten used to it. This time though, he sounded upset. He was looking at the screen on his desk; the one that has little pads that he taps on endlessly for hours.

"Are you freaking kidding me?" He turned and looked at Hoppi as she walked into the room.

"I sent out my latest newsletter. I reviewed it probably four or five times. I just noticed—after I published it—an error. In the *first line* of the newsletter. Darn it! How did that happen? All those great resources—twenty-five of them!—I included will be overshadowed by that stupid mistake!"

He carried on and on about this *error* worse than if he caught me peeing in the house. (Which of course I had not done since I was an awkward little puppy, thank you.) Hoppi did what she could to calm him down—but he persisted in yelling at himself.

Finally, he looked at me. "Roxie, let's go for a walk." I was down with that and ran behind him to the leash and out the door.

He kept muttering to himself about the *error*. I didn't get it. At all. And he was just working himself up into a state. While I had no idea what the *error* was about, I could tell he wasn't going to let this go. And it was affecting our walk time as he was walking quickly and starting to pull a bit too hard on the leash.

I finally just stopped hard and pulled back. That caught his attention. I looked at him.

Look, I said to him with my eyes, *you made an error. Look at the big picture. I heard you say you just sent out a newsletter with great resources relating to growth and resilience. If someone gets whacked about a small error—and does not even see the good stuff you provided—then maybe you don't need that unforgiving person on your list.*

And humans sometimes call us dumb animals. Geez.

There are beings who live to tell everyone else what they did wrong—while they risk little. We should be happy that we did, or at least attempted to do, something worthwhile.

My gosh, where would I have been if I did not come out of my crates or off my fluff pillows and explore. At times, I was anxious, but I learned a lot. Sometimes I made mistakes. Like when Steve threw a ball, I ran to it, and then went off and peed. But all was good. Life went on.

We finished our walk, and Steve had calmed down. I heard him tell Hoppi as he settled back into his chair behind the screen with little pads for his fingers to touch, "I think Roxie was trying to remind me, with those big brown eyes, that I cannot let perfection and disappointment rule. I cannot let the fear of being wrong, making a misstep or committing a mistake, keep me from doing stuff."

Whatever that means.

But it seemed to calm him down. That was good. And, I curled up and faded off to sleep under his desk.

Beyond the Biscuit

Think about the last time you did something that made another person's life better—even if just a little bit. What did you do? How did the person feel? How did you feel?

SPOILED?

HOW CAN YOU CREATE A LIFE FILLED WITH LOVE, HEALTH, DISCIPLINE, RELATIONSHIPS, CARE, ATTENTION, AND PURPOSE?

Most mornings, after Steve and I finish our morning stretches and meditation session, we make our way to the beach for sunrise. One of the things I enjoy about these walks is meeting up with my canine buddies. Baby, Maker's, Bear, Cotton, Dino, Dash, Coco, Gigi, and Tater Tot make up the regulars. We do the doggie handshake, jump around, and enjoy the company. Not once have we ever exchanged a cross utterance. Civility at its best. Steve refers to me as the Best Dog Ever, but truth be told, my buds are awesome themselves.

And, Steve always has a pocket full of biscuits for my buds and me. Yum!

On a recent walk, I heard one of the humans say, "Roxie is the most spoiled dog on the block."

Spoiled?

Not sure what that word means. So, as Steve and I sat on the beach, I tried to figure it out. What would make me *spoiled?* What do the neighbors see that would lead to that conclusion? I thought of my life and thought *spoiled* must mean:

- Never having a cross interaction with another being.
- Getting affectionate touches from humans.
- Going on two or three great walks a day on the beach and in the park.
- Visiting the local dog park and having "sleep overs" at the little yellow building.
- Being served nutritious and tasty food each day. (Yum, yum, yum!)
- Enjoying "couch time" at night with my people.
- Getting a treat now and then.
- Sharing a treat with my canine buddies.
- Having comfortable beds to rest, sleep, and dream upon.
- Receiving consistent love and attention from Steve and Hoppi.
- Being regularly bathed and cared for.
- Having all my shots up to date.
- Reading with elementary school children.
- Visiting high school students to help them during exams.
- Having a backyard so that I can enjoy nature.
- Sleeping as needed.
- Following commands from my person and being respectful.
- Bringing a smile to the faces of people who may need a healing touch.
- And, of course, receiving a biscuit or two from time to time.

So, does Love + Health + Discipline + Relationships + Care + Attention + Purpose = Spoiled?

As the sun popped up over the ocean, I thought if that is being *spoiled* then I like it. Yes, I guess I am *spoiled*, and I hope my canine buds (and their humans) are *spoiled* as well.

Woof!

Beyond the Biscuit

What does *spoiled* mean to you? Are you spoiled? If not, would you like to be? What is attractive about being spoiled? Are there any challenges with being spoiled?

LEAN IN

HOW CAN WE CREATE AN ENVIRONMENT THAT PROMOTES NO BARKING, NO JUMPING, NO RUDENESS, NO SHOWBOATING, NO UGLINESS, AND NO PUT-DOWNS?

Every week, Steve takes me to visit people in a big building. Well, there are a few big buildings he takes me to.

I know when the day comes. My first clue is my bath. I must always be clean before I go to the buildings. Before we leave the house, he will wrap a vest or bandana around my body. He positions it just so and snugs it to fit comfortably. He then adds another jingle to my collar in the shape of a read heart. He puts some tags on a long rope for himself and hangs them around his neck. And off we go for our adventure.

I have come to learn that one of the buildings we visit is where people *come to go*, and the other is a place they *come to stay*.

In the *come to go* place, there are more people than I have ever seen at one time. They all drag bags on wheels behind them. They stand in long lines, take off their shoes, and belts, and then hold their hands over their heads. Then they put their shoes and belts back on and stand in another line where they get something handed to them in a cup. Then off they go down the hall and sit.

Outside the windows, I can see the biggest machines ever. Much bigger than Steve's car. And a lot louder.

At some point, the people get up, walk through another door, the door closes, and I never see the people or their bags again. I heard Steve say one time that sometimes those people never see their bags again either.

Whatever.

As Steve and I walk around the building, people stop to talk and rub my back, scratch my butt, or if I'm lucky, massage my belly. My favorite! They can find me easily for two reasons. One, I am a dog, and two, both Steve and I wear blue vests so that we stand out a bit from the rest of the people.

Poor Steve, though, as it seems everybody looks at me and calls my name. No one ever scratches his ears or rubs his belly. I feel like no one knows him. But he seems OK with it. He's good that way.

All my friendships start with someone looking, and then smiling, as we walk by. Steve walks us to the person. There is a paw shake or body language welcoming an interaction. They smile, and then they start to talk. Like we are old friends.

I hear them talk about their dogs, family, home, and why they *come to go.* It's like as soon as I approach, they start to talk and laugh. I do not interrupt. I let them speak. I really don't understand their words. And sometimes the words are very different from group to group. Like another language. Other than seeing a gentle stroke in my future, I carry no prejudgments.

I, also, have met new friends in the place people *come to stay.* Rather than a vest, I wear a bandana around by neck and a tag with my photo hangs from my collar. I look pretty darn official.

The place where people *come to stay* is closer to home. We visit people in offices and some in hallways. Unlike the other building, there are no bags on wheels. But there are wheels.

Often, I will see a bed on wheels. Someone pushes it, and someone lays on top of it. Usually sleeping. Sometimes people sit in chairs with wheels and, again, someone pushes them. I don't know where they go.

Steve pushes a button on a wall, a door opens, we walk in, the door closes, and there we are in what feels like a small closet. And then the closet starts to move. Next thing I know, the door opens, and we walk out to a different floor from where the door closed. Steve is good at this kind of surprise.

On these floors there are a lot of people in beds. Some look asleep. Others stare at a screen on the wall kind of like what Steve and Hoppi have at home that they stare at. Sometimes they laugh and other times they might even yell at the screen. Seems silly but if it makes them happy, that's ok.

We stop and visit people. Some pet me. Some just look at me and smile. Some cry.

Like the day we were walking in the place people *come to stay*, and we saw a woman walking toward us. I wasn't paying much attention as I was searching the floor for news. Then I heard the woman speak to Steve, though I saw she was looking at me.

"I need to pet a dog at this moment," she said.

As she neared us, I noticed she had a clump of papers in her hand. With her other hand, she reached out to me. I walked and stood beside her and gently leaned into her as she stroked my back with a soft hand. Back and forth. I thought I felt something wet on my back, but I wasn't sure. As she continued talking, her fingers moved back and forth on my fur.

"I just learned I have a brain tumor." She kept contact with my back. She and Steve spoke, though she did most of the speaking in a soft voice.

I listened. It sounded like she was sad. And her hand never left my back. I continued to lean into her.

A few minutes later, the woman excused herself and disappeared behind a door. Before she left, she raised her eyes from me, looked at Steve, and said she believed the universe brought the three of us together at that point in time.

I don't know what any of it meant. I noticed Steve had a sad smile. As the lady left, he knelt beside me and hugged me.

"Good girl, Roxie. You helped that woman. She needed to talk. You did more for her than I could have by myself." He stroked my head.

"We would all be better off if we were like you, Roxie. No barking. No jumping. No rudeness. No showboating. No ugliness. No put-downs. Just being there. This is our purpose, Roxie."

At times people cry. Other times they smile and speak. Whatever they do, I listen and lean in.

Beyond the Biscuit

At times, we seem to be in the right place at the right time for the right people. Describe a time when you found yourself in such a position.

THE ANXIOUS TRAVELER

WHO CAME TO YOUR SIDE TO HELP YOU
THROUGH A DIFFICULT TIME?

I've come to learn that whether I go to the building people *come to go* or *come to stay*, I have a job. Or, at least, that's what I hear Steve say.

"You gotta work tomorrow, Roxie."

Not sure what *work* means, but every time he says that, I can count on our routine. Even though I've shared this with you in a previous story, I'd like to woof a little more about bath time.

When it is warm outside, he uses the tube attached to the house, out of which comes water. Other times, we do this inside. He opens the clear sliding doors in his and Hoppi's potty room. I walk in and sit. He never has to ask twice. I love it! Warm water, soft white fluffy foam that coats me, and the massage. I mean, come on, Steve rubs the fluffy foam into my fur over my whole body. How could you *not* like that?

After he rinses me, he briskly rubs me down with warm dry towels.

"You smell good, Doodles! You are ready for your *job* tomorrow."

One day, when we were at the building that people *come to go*, one of the men in an official looking outfit came up and spoke to Steve.

"Hey, would you mind taking the pup over to gate C4? We have a traveler who is having an anxiety attack."

Although I tilted my head to look like I was following the conversation, the truth is the only thing I focused on was that he called me a *pup*. Wasn't sure if I should be offended or not. I choose to take it as a compliment. He thought of me as young at heart!

We made our way to C4. There we found two older people. The man stood, and the woman knelt on one leg. Both looked sad as they were talking to a younger woman sitting in a chair with wheels on it.

"We just got here for our flight, and she is a bit nervous," said the older woman as she gently touched the woman sitting in the chair with wheels.

I had never heard *nervous* before. And if this was *nervous*, well, wow! The younger woman had lots of water coming from her eyes. When Steve first tried to speak to her, all she did was look toward the floor. She looked so sad.

"Hi! This is Roxie. She wanted to say hello to you."

Hearing my name caught my attention. Then he gently moved me closer to the chair with wheels on it so that my head was close to the young woman.

"You can pet Roxie if you want to. She would like that."

I sat there and watched her. Steve engaged her in some conversation, and slowly she turned toward me with her eyes.

"Will Roxie go on the flight with me?" she asked.

I heard my name and wiggled a bit.

"No, Roxie will stay with me. She would be happy if you would like to pet her. Would you like that?"

The younger woman in the chair with wheels on it glanced toward me and ever so slowly moved her hand to the top of my head and softly rubbed. It felt nice.

Steve spoke with the older man and woman. He spoke some more with the younger woman petting my head. I noticed the water had stopped falling from her eyes.

"Thank you for letting Roxie visit with you," Steve said. "I know you have to get ready for your flight. You really made Roxie feel good today."

And she did.
And I did.
And she smiled.
And so did Steve.

Beyond the Biscuit

Perhaps there have been times when you were nervous about something. It could have been because of something at work, school, or home. Whatever it was, you might have found yourself unable to effectively deal with it. Who came to your side to help you through? What did that person do? How did it help you?

THE GARNASIUM

WHAT EXERCISE AND MINDFULNESS ROUTINES START YOUR DAY?

S teve and Hoppi have a sweet crate themselves. It's not as nice as mine—but it is bigger. While it sits higher off the floor than my crate, theirs doesn't have any sides or a door. Just a lot of pillows and sheets. They don't seem to be afraid of falling out or anything getting in, though.

And it smells so good in the room. Like the plants I've buried my nose in our walks. The ones with tall bluish flowers. I'm so glad they have allowed my crate to sit in one corner of their crate room. As it should be. We are family, after all.

Steve has a calming way to end one day and begin the next. After I walk into my crate, the last thing he does is scratch my haunches, gently latch the crate door, and say, "Night, Roxie."

The next morning, he quietly opens my crate and says, "Morning, Roxie." And then I get nose-nuzzle time before he lets me outside for my morning potty break. I'm not sure but I think while I'm outside, Steve takes his own potty break, inside the house. He puts lights on for me outside as we are usually up and out of our crates a long time before we see the sunlight. Peaceful time when not many others are walking around.

When he lets me back in, we both spend time in what he calls his Garnasium. I have not heard any of his friends talk about them having a Garnasium. I guess we are special. Some might call this a garage, but we don't park cars here. Steve has put a lot of toys that he plays with each morning. I get to watch all he does while I lay on the floor, head between my legs, and my eyes following his every move. Until I decide to take a short power nap.

He first gets on a one-wheeled bike. It does not go anyplace. He pumps the handles and peddles back-and-forth while sitting on a seat. The one wheel makes a roaring noise and it creates a lot of air. The wind feels cool.

When he steps off the bike, he stretches his arms over his head, behind his back, and down to his toes. He lays on the floor and grunts as he tries to sit up and touch his elbows to his knees. He grunts a lot. He stretches his legs using a long rope. He really grunts when he does that.

Off to the side of the bike with one wheel rest his stupid bells. Well, I wouldn't say they're stupid, and I certainly would not call them bells, as they do not ring or clang. But Steve insists on calling them his "dumbbells." And he calls me a doodle!

Anyway, somedays he lifts the stupid bells starting with the little ones and ending with bigger ones. And at times, he reverses, starting with the big stupid bells and moving to the smaller stupid ones. Again, lots of grunting. About this time, I usually stretch, re-position myself, and nap some more. I am just glad to be with him and not have to do any of the work he is grunting over.

When he is done, he dims the lights, sits on the floor cross-legged, and closes his eyes for a while. Very peaceful feeling.

Oh, and there is music too. I never see him turn the music on. He—and this is a bit strange—talks to someone who is not in the room. And then, just like a treat appearing from his pocket, the music starts to play. Really! I've heard it so much, I know it by heart.

"Alexa. Play meditation music."

A woman speaks back, and then there is music! Steve is so good.

About the time Steve opens his eyes and bows toward the floor, I can see some light starting to peek through the Garnasium window. I get up because I know what is next.

"Thanks for keeping me company, Roxie. How about we go to the beach?"

He puts a fistful of biscuits into his pocket for our walk (and for my buds we will see on the sand) and leashes me up; we turn off the lights as we close the door and head out the gate.

Everyone should be able to start a day in a Garnasium.

Beyond the Biscuit

How do you start your day? What exercise and mindfulness routines do you have? How do they help you stay focused on your purpose?

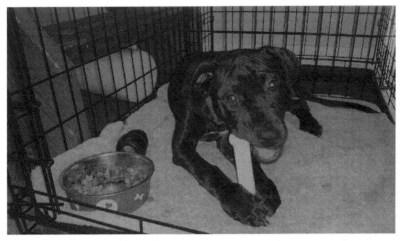

My first puppy condo.

Chilling at sunrise.

Seriously? Another photo?

Need I say more?

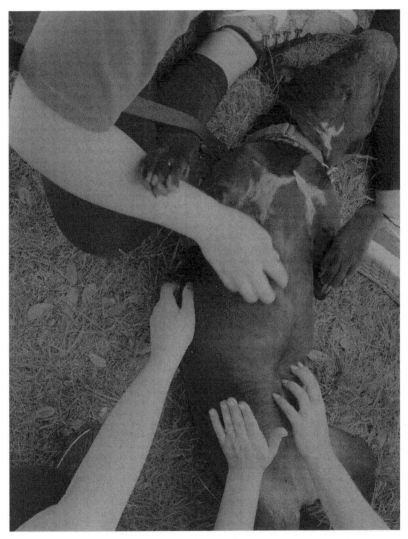

Life is good!

Here's looking at you!

Power naps are a good thing!

EXPLORING.
CONNECTING. CHILLING.

DOES YOUR CURIOSITY ENCOURAGE YOU TO PAUSE AND APPRECIATE? OR DO YOU MISS WHAT IS IN YOUR PRESENT MOMENT AS YOU HURRY ON TO YOUR FUTURE MOMENTS?

A s you have gathered by now, I like to take my time with things. Whether in the backyard, out for a walk, or on the beach, my paws and nose keep me in the present moment.

For instance, on a recent beach walk, we stumbled across more shells (and a few stinky dead fish) on the beach than I had ever seen. From shells as small as one of my paw pads to a few that were bigger than my head, I saw all sorts of colors, sizes, and shapes. Far too many to just go prancing by them. I had to encourage Steve to stop and smell the seashells. I went into full nose-to-ground mode. Wow! So much to wrap my little pulsating nostrils around.

A word about odors. My nose leads me to explore. I want to know who has been there before me and how long ago it might have been since they visited that spot. Who knows, one of my canine buds might have left a message for me. The strength or weakness of the odor gives clues. Often, I will leave a message myself. Steve and his human friends *look* a lot at the world. Us dogs can't help but *smell* a lot of the world. So, when we came across all those shells on the sand, well, it was like a party. What may be odoriferous to a human is a wonderful smorgasbord for a dog. (Like that? A vocabulary twofer!)

A little further down the sand we ran into one of my pup friends, Tater Tot, and her person, Roz. Tater Tot is much smaller than me; she sits pretty low to the ground. I remember when we first met, she wanted to remain close to Roz. Tater Tot wasn't too sure about me. Steve helped win her over with a biscuit from his pocket. Now whenever we see each other, I play bow and then raise up on my hind legs in greeting. Tater Tot acknowledges me but really has eyes for Steve. More specifically, eyes for his biscuit pocket. That's OK, as Roz has biscuits she shares with me. Everyone is happy! Always fun to connect with little TT.

While I love exploring and connecting, my favorite thing to do on the beach is to paw away a little bit of sand, lay on my belly, and stretch out my legs as far as they will go. I just take in the sounds, smells, people, birds, and the water. Chill time. I watch other dogs run, jump, and dig. They look like they are having fun. I lay there. Some might call me lazy. I prefer to call it economy of motion.

There is one dog I have seen on the beach often with her person. Rather than lie in the sand, this dog digs. And digs. And. Digs. I've never witnessed so much sand flying! And when she finishes that hole, she begins another. She goes deep, like almost up to her hind quarters. Lots of work. I lay there and admire her work from afar. I could do that too, but why? I don't like unnecessary movement. Again, economy of motion seems more my lifestyle choice.

Exploring, connecting, and chilling. A dog's life is pretty good. At least, this dog's life is.

Beyond the Biscuit

How often do you explore where you live? I mean really explore and get curious about what you see? I wonder at times if Steve sees what we pass on each walk. I know he can see with his eyes. I wonder, though, how much appreciation he has for what he takes in with his eyes and nose.

When you go for a walk, does your curiosity about what is in front of you cause you to pause and appreciate? Or do you focus on something else, missing what you *for sure* have in front of you on your way to *what might be* in your future?

FOCUS ON THE PRESENT

HOW DO YOU BALANCE BETWEEN FOCUSING ON THE FUTURE AND APPRECIATING THE PRESENT?

One day, as we walked through the big building where people *come to go*, I heard my name from behind, which was not unusual. Like I've mentioned before, people seem to know my name but not Steve's. He doesn't seem to mind.

"Roxie! Roxie!"

We turned and saw a petite woman approaching us. I recognized her as one of the women who, standing behind a counter on the side of the hallway, talked to people as they passed by. We stopped and waited for her.

"You walked by so fast that I did not have a chance to touch Roxie." She knelt and rubbed my back and scratched my ears. She had a nice smile.

Steve promised to walk slower on our next visit.

That got me thinking about one of the things on which Steve and I differ.

Focus.

Now, don't get me wrong. He is a focused guy. He works hard at his machine with those little pads that he taps with his fingers, and he works a lot around the house. And at night, he sometimes goes out to do work with his neighbors.

But he always seems to be focused on where he is going; where he needs to be; or what he needs to get done.

For me, I focus on where I am. The smells in front or to the side of me or the cool sand on my body. In the park, I'll stop just to stare at the turtles or ducks in the park. If a cat is nearby, I want to go up and get to know it. Of course, the cats are so arrogant and self-righteous. They ignore me. That's another story.

If I see something laying by the side of the road, I want to explore it. Another dog comes by, I want to stop and exchange a doggie handshake.

I don't want to miss a thing. If it was put in my path, I believe it was put there for a reason. I must explore what surrounds me. Get to know it well.

Steve's focus on our walks is often where we are going. He wants to *arrive at* the beach. Or *get around* the park and *return* home. I know he has a lot on his mind. Humans are always so busy. But he misses so much along the way.

I'd like to tell him to slow down. But I can't speak. So, I use my body if I really think we need to pay attention to something near us. I will just stop and give a little pull on the leash. Steve stops and looks at me, and then we both get to look at what he has missed because he is focused on the future.

He is a work in progress. And I see improvement.

Good, Steve! Good, person!

Beyond the Biscuit

How do you keep balance between focusing on the future (where you are going; where you need to be; or what you need to get done) and appreciation for the present (what is in front of you)?

SERVICE AS PURPOSE

IF SOMEONE ASKED YOU, "WHAT IS YOUR PURPOSE?" WHAT WOULD YOU SAY?

When Steve and I travel to the places where people *come to go* and *come to stay*, we have a name. Kind of like a work title. More specifically, what we do has a name. It is, I believe, our purpose for getting ready, jumping in the car, and walking around the buildings. Come to think of it, that is why we spent so much time with Bill, Marcie, and Stacy.

Pet Therapy. I hear Steve use those words a lot. When we meet someone and they approach me, he helps them understand what we do. He usually says something like,

> *Hi. This is Roxie and we are part of the pet therapy team. Roxie is here to bring smiles to faces and hear you speak. She is a conversation starter. You can pet Roxie if you would like.*

People smile and, as I have said in a few of my earlier stories, they not only pet and rub me, they begin to talk about animals in their lives. There are always grins and laughs. I like my purpose.

I find it interesting that Steve never talks about himself. I mean, without him, we would not be in front of those people as I can't drive. But he always makes the visit about me and the person touching me. That's just how Steve rolls.

Although it may look like I am always on the hunt for food on the floor, I pay attention to what and who is around me. That is how I have come to understand that there are other dog-human teams that have a purpose. Some are pet therapy teams and others are not. Steve will also talk about this with people as we visit.

For instance, often the first question a person asks is, "May I touch your dog?" Or, I have heard mommies tell their little humans, "Oh, you can't touch that dog, dear. He is working."

While I am going to share a little bit about these different types of teams, I also will share something you can listen to. One day, Steve spoke with another very nice lady who spoke a lot about what animals can do to help people. I was in the room when they spoke. At the end of this story, I will tell you how you can find out more information from this nice lady about animals.

And, that will be my first footnote, thank you. Hanging around Steve, I've learned about proper citations. You're welcome.

While we are a *pet therapy* team, there are other types of dogs doing special jobs as well.

Working Dogs. I have seen these dogs and their humans mostly at the place people *come to go.* Their humans often dress in a uniform, and the dogs usually have a vest around their chest and back. They sniff and move about. Like I do. But differently. They smell the bags on wheels that people carry. At times, they stop and put their noses close to the people's bodies and clothes. Mostly, they move from person to person without much happening. However, if they stop and stay with a bag or person that usually means they found something that should not be in the place where people *come to go.*

You cannot touch these dogs. I cannot touch them, either. Not only can I not do the doggie handshake with them, Steve and I have been asked to move to the other side of the building if one of these dogs is sniffing. No one ever clears a room for my sniffing. These are special dogs, and they serve an important purpose keeping people safe.

Service Dogs. Most times, these dogs have a vest on as well. Their person generally looks like other people in the room. That is, no special uniform. I have come to learn that when these dogs are present, I need to ignore them and so do other people. My purpose is to let people touch me. I am there for them—all of them. The service dog's purpose is to serve the person it is with. No one else is to touch a service dog. These dogs can help calm down their person or help the person walk or pick up something. These dogs are protective of and serve their people.

The best rule of paw when you meet up with a dog is to always ask the person with the animal if it is ok to touch or pet it. Never assume it is ok for you to start playing with the canine. Always ask.

Beyond the Biscuit

If someone came up to you and asked you, "What is your purpose?" how would you answer?

Here is the footnote I promised: Steve Piscitelli, "How Can You Help Heal the World?" Episode #36 on The Growth and Resilience Network® podcast channel. A conversation with the Reverend Elizabeth Teal. https://www.youtube.com/watch?v=C9z F8alyxVk&feature=youtu.be. May 15, 2018.

SNIFFS, SMELLS, SOUNDS, AND SNIPS

WHEN WAS THE LAST TIME YOU WENT THROUGH SOME PAIN IN ORDER TO FEEL BETTER?

As I've noted in other stories, I enjoy touching and being touched.

Steve and I start each day with a nose nuzzle and belly rub. It's how we say good morning. Well, I get the belly rub, not Steve.

I assume all humans greet the day and the humans they live with in the same manner. Kind and loving recognition. I see Steve and Hoppi start each day with a little nose nuzzle. Though, I confess, I've not seen much belly rubbing. Maybe they hide that from me, so I don't get jealous.

One morning, Steve was paying more attention than normal to one of my ears.

"Did you see this?" Hoppi leaned in and rubbed it gently. It did not hurt me, and the ear rub was kind of nice.

"Looks like a wart."

I kind of remembered that word when I had my mouth problems a few years back.

Later that day, Steve took me to Dr. Moody. I knew exactly where I was from the smells. They are all around. Starting with around the outside of the building. Lots of scents in the grass, on the plants, and sprayed up on the outside walls. I could smell cats and dogs. A lot of them. When we walked inside, I was greeted with even more smells. In addition to cats and dogs, I could smell food. I could tell where some past visitors may have used the cool floor to relieve themselves. Some scents told me animals may have been a bit scared. Not sure of what. Every time I've been there has been pleasant, although occasionally I do get stuck with a needle or two. And, I always get a biscuit on my way out the door.

No needles this time as all eyes and hands were on my ear. Steve and Dr. Moody talked briefly, and we left. After I got a biscuit, of course.

A few days later, we returned.

We were led into a smaller room by a young woman with a nice smile. As we waited for Dr. Moody, I could hear a cat from the other side of the door. It was meowing like it was scared. I tilted my head and lifted my ears to hear as much as I could. I sat there totally focused on what was happening on the other side of the door.

Then Dr. Moody came in and spoke briefly to Steve. The young woman returned and took my leash and told Steve to have a seat. Guess, you can say this was kind of a *Sit Steve, sit.* And he did.

Good Steve, good!

I pranced into the next room taking in all the sniffs, smells, and sounds. They lifted me on to a table. The young woman gave me a big warm hug. It felt good and I....

Hey. Ouch!

I felt a sting in my ear.

"That's OK, Roxie. It'll be OK."

Then my ear kind of went numb. All I knew was that Dr. Moody was playing with it. I felt a little tug, a rub, and pull. No pain, though.

What's that smell?

I could sniff a whiff of something singeing. And that was it. I was led back to the room where Steve was waiting.

"She'll be fine. Keep the ear dry for a few days." Dr Moody handed the leash back to Steve.

They spoke a little more. I heard something about no pet therapy this week. We walked out. I got a biscuit. I felt good.

Beyond the Biscuit

This story reminds me that sometimes we must endure a little pain in order to feel a little better in the long run. When was the last time you went through some pain in order to feel better? What advice would you give to someone who might be fearful of doing something that, in the short term might cause some discomfort, but in the long term would be much better for his/her wellbeing?

WHAT ARE YOU THINKING?

HAVE YOU EVER EXPERIENCED FEAR OR ANXIETY WHEN MEETING A NEW GROUP OF PEOPLE?

Steve and I have two predictable paths we walk in the park across from our house. One leads us to the beach and the other around the park. One is our morning path and the other our afternoon stroll.

One morning, I thought he was lost. We had walked through the park, and I could sense the beach up ahead. But instead of going straight, we moved to the right, on to a concrete path alongside the road. At first, I stopped, figuring he was once again thinking about something other than our walk. He must have turned the wrong way. I tilted my head and looked at him.

"Come on, Roxie, today we're going to school." He smiled and scratched my ear.

School? I had not heard that word before. I followed.

Just a few minutes later, I saw this brightly colored pink building with grass and cars. And a lot of people walking in the front door. By now, I was used to going into buildings with lots of people.

This was different, though. Most of the people were little. As in small. As in young.

We walked up the steps and through the front door on to the shiny cool floor and then into a room with a counter. I could not see the people over the counter. Steve stopped, and I sat beside him.

"Hi, this is Roxie. We are here to visit Ms. Moran's class."

A kindly lady peered over the counter and smiled when she saw me looking up at her. I know how to use my eyes, if you know what I mean. She told us where the room was, and off we went.

By now, as we walked on the inside of the building, I did not see many people—big or little. We walked by a lot of doors, and I could hear people talking, some loudly. But they all appeared happy; lots of laughing. Some singing. I smelled good smells.

Seems like a nice enough place, I thought.

It was certainly different than the place Steve and I visit every week where people *come to stay*. I could sense the playful energy in this building. And there were no bags on wheels like we see every time we go to the place people *come to go*.

We stopped at a door, and I sat as he knocked.

"OK, Roxie. This is Ms. Moran's kindergarten class. Her students will be so happy to meet you."

Kindergarten? What, we are at a garden?

Again, I was lost. Steve handed me a biscuit. I was good! Kindergarten here I come.

A nice young woman with the biggest smile I had ever seen opened the door and greeted us.

"We are so glad you and Roxie have come today. The children can't wait to visit with you. Come on in, they are waiting."

She held the door open. We stepped in and were immediately greeted with more excitement than I ever heard anywhere—even back in my puppy room days. And, louder than the little yellow building where I play with my canine buds.

"Class. This is Mr. Piscitelli, and this is Roxie." She pointed to me. And then the little people moved toward me. Like a huge wave I would see on the beach! They smiled, laughed, and giggled. They were all talking at once. I looked up at Steve as I took a step backward.

Where in the world have you taken me? What are you thinking?

Ms. Moran stepped in front of us.

"Class, we don't want to scare Roxie, do we?"

"No, ma'am."

"Let's all move to the carpet and sit down. You will all have a chance to pet Roxie, but we must be gentle and only a few of you at a time. We want her to feel comfortable here."

With that, all the little humans moved to a soft rug.

"Criss-cross apple sauce!" I heard Ms. Moran say. And with that they all sat and crossed their legs. And they were quiet. Pretty cool. I liked Ms. Moran. My protector!

In front of them was a big chair that Ms. Moran led us to. She really knew how to handle her little people. I wondered if they were all hers. But figured not. She was far too young to have such a big litter of pups.

Steve sat down in the chair. He knew I was feeling a bit out of my element, if you know what I mean. He held the leash in one hand and gently stroked my head and back with the other. I heard him tell the little people how he and I met, where we lived, and some of the things we did and places we visited. The first row of children was close enough to touch me, but they did not because Ms. Moran had told them not yet.

That is when I noticed a space under the chair Steve was sitting on. I crawled under as far as I could go. Got about halfway; my backside was still visible. I needed some space!

I heard Steve reading a story, and then I felt it.

A little hand was touching my butt. Softly going back and forth. It was nice. Then there was another hand, and another. All stroking my fur.

Steve encouraged me to come out. I don't remember, but there was probably a biscuit involved. Anyway, when I backed out, I saw the little people looking at me.

"OK, class," Ms. Moran said, "let's switch rows. Those in the font move to the back. We all want a chance to love on Roxie."

With that the children traded places, and a new set of hands rubbed on me.

OK! I like this!

By the time Steve finished reading, and all the little people had had a chance to sit in the front row, it was time for us to leave. Ms. Moran thanked us for coming, and they gave me a gift. A stuffed toy. Wow! I didn't see that coming. Cool.

The little people all stood in a straight line, and as we walked out of the room, they said goodbye and stroked my back. One little person leaned over and hugged me.

We stopped at the door. Steve waved. And out we walked.

I didn't know what Steve was thinking when he brought me to these little people. But I was glad he did. He helped me stretch my comfort zone one more time. The energy was good in Ms. Moran's room. I remember the hug and soft touches. And, I think in some small way, I may have helped the little people that day.

"Thank you, Roxie. You did well. You made a lot of people smile today." And with that, Steve smiled, and I got a biscuit. Yum!

Beyond the Biscuit

At first, I was scared when I entered Ms. Moran's room. But because of Steve and Ms. Moran, I learned to like where I was and all those little people I met. I gave them a chance and got to know them a little better. I found them to be kind.

Think of a time when you found yourself nervous about being in a new place with people you did not know. How did you get over the initial fear? How did you give them a chance to show their kindness? Who helped you? Have you helped someone who was fearful because she was new to a group? What kind things did you do or gentle words did you speak?

DOGSPLAINING

WHY DO YOU THINK IT IS DIFFICULT FOR SOME PEOPLE TO ADMIT THEIR MISTAKES?

By now, you know that Steve and I are tight. We spend a lot of time together. He understands me. Like when I quietly sit by the door, he knows I would like to go outside. Those times I put my head in his lap as he is at his desk, he understands that it's time for a walk. He takes care of me and will do anything for me. It's cool how we can communicate without speaking a word.

There have been times, though, that I wish I could have done more than give him a look or tug on the leash. Even more than an impatient bark or a whimper—which I am hesitant to do. Not very dignified. But, you see, there are times when humans just don't know what it is like to be a dog. Even though they supposedly have superior intellect, there are a few topics I'd like to do some *dogsplaining*. Here is one they need help with.

I wish humans could walk in our paws for a day. Literally. Especially on a hot day. When they take us for a walk. On. Hot. Pavement. Let me give you an example.

One morning, Steve and I had just made our last visit at the place people *come to stay* and left the building to go home. We had brought smiles to a lot of people, and I got a few biscuits along the way. As we walked through the door, I could feel it immediately. From the cool inside to the hot outside. Very hot. Steve had parked the car in the big lot for cars. The big *black* lot. The big *black and hot* lot.

I know Steve was hot like me as he was walking quickly to the car. But unlike me, he had shoes on his feet. I did not. And that is something humans might miss. Our paws can be tender.

I pride myself on my toughness. But on that day, my paws were feeling the sizzle of the *black and hot* lot. I pulled Steve toward the first car I saw.

"Not that one, Rox. Our car is a little further." And with that, he tugged on the lead and we walked on. He thought I had forgotten what our ride looked like. He did not understand my signal.

I dutifully followed his lead but with each step my paw pads were starting to sting. I wish I could have yelled, *Hey, my paws are burning up!*

I eventually had to take the leash into my own paws. I pulled hard left to a patch of grass that was behind the parked cars. I looked at Steve. He returned my gaze. I think he finally got it.

He followed me to the grass. From there we navigated to the car. I jumped in, stretched out on the back seat, and felt cold air blowing from the front. Much better.

When we got home, Steve was rubbing me down like he usually does. I rolled over for a much-needed belly rub. And that is when he saw my paws.

"Oh, Roxie, I am sorry. That's why you were pulling me. Your paws look a little rough. I wasn't fast enough."

Well, he was fast, just not quick enough. Humans do not understand how quickly our paws can feel the sting of heat.

The next day we visited the same nice lady who helped when I had those fleshy warts on my mouth a few years ago. She examined my paws, suggested some lotion to rub on them, and told Steve I would be OK. Nothing serious, though there were a few raw spots. She suggested he get me some paw coverings.

The next day, Steve had a present for me. He called them *socks*. For a few nights, after he'd gently rub soothing liquid on my paws, he would slip the socks over my paws. I know he meant well, but these blasted things took a bit of getting used to. Most mornings, when he let me out of the crate, the socks were in a pile on the floor. When we went for our first walk with them on my paws, you would have thought I was learning to walk. They felt nice and soft, but I was not used to anything on my paws. Kind of constricting if you know what I mean. Steve showed patience and slowed our pace so we could get around the park.

My paws quickly healed, and the socks were washed and placed in the same drawer as my Garnasium biscuits. (Not sure I mentioned it before, but I have upstairs biscuits, bedroom biscuits, and Garnasium biscuits. Steve controls the delivery. But I know where they are.)

I have noticed that I get the socks more often when we walk on hot days. In fact, our afternoon walks have been postponed to later in the day when it's cooler. And he keeps me on grass or sand.

One day, I saw him place his hand on the road outside our house.

"Hoppi said if it's too hot for me to hold my hand there, then it is too hot for you to walk, Roxie."

Hoppi is one smart human!

On that day in the parking lot, Steve had made a mistake, and he learned a valuable lesson. He never made that mistake again. I am glad that he pays attention and is a quick study.

Beyond the Biscuit

Making a mistake is easy to do. Admitting to that mistake, learning from it, and not repeating it, can be more difficult. We must move beyond simply saying, "I'm sorry." We must figure out how to correct the situation and make it better. When was the last time you made a mistake and owned it? What lesson did you learn? Why do you think it is difficult for some people to admit their mistakes?

TREAT ME WELL, AND I WANT TO TREAT YOU BETTER

WHY WOULD ANYONE WANT TO SPEAK TO SOMEONE WHO WILL NOT LISTEN?

I need to clarify something. Not everyone at the place where people *come to stay* always stay. I have noted that many *come to work*. Some work behind screens and tap on keys, like Steve does in my office at home. (Oh, excuse me. I meant to say *Steve's* office.)

Others tend to the people who do *come to stay*. These people dress in crisp colored uniforms: blue, purple, green, gray, and white. They carry things in and out of rooms for the people who have *come to stay*. Sometimes they are pushing people who sit or lay on things with wheels. They attach tubes to some people and help others stand and walk. They never seem to stop working.

Steve and I spend a lot of time visiting with these humans. The ones wearing blue are called nurses. Hoppi used to work as a nurse in the place people *come to stay*.

Steve always asks if there are certain humans who might like a visit from us. Often, nurses look at him and say, "I need the visit."

They then rub my back and talk to me. They always smile and thank me for visiting.

One day, I heard one of the people in a uniform say her day had not been a good one. She bent down and hugged me for a few moments. She smiled, thanked me, and walked away. The smile is all I need. Their kind touches are good, too.

There are others who call my name when they see me. A few even have biscuits hidden away in a bag for me. Yum! I have come to know exactly where they are stashed. I'm pretty observant, you know.

While I love visiting all the people—those who *come to stay* and those who *come to work*—I do get tired after we have been visiting for a while. I let Steve know by slowing my pace or just looking at him.

I love this. But I'm dog-tired.

He will motivate me with one word. You guessed it: "Biscuit!" Up I'll jump. Good for a few more minutes.

"This is our last stop today, Roxie. We won't stay long. You know they love to see you."

I recognized this building because it has doors that automatically swing out when we approach. We don't have to stop and open them. We just walk right in.

In this particular place, I see old humans and very young humans. Some so young that they are still held by their mamas. The mamas, many times, have a worried look on their faces. They might just be tired. I don't know.

This day there was one young human who caught my attention. She stood a little taller than me, had curly hair, and wore eyeglasses. They were like what Steve wears at night around our house. I had never seen such a little human with eyeglasses. And she also wore a big bright smile.

I saw Steve speaking with her mama, and then he knelt down next me, put his hand on my chest, and spoke to the little person.

"This is Roxie. Would you like to pet her? Roxie would like it if you want to."

The little girl let go of her mama's hand and walked straight to me. She slowly stretched her hand toward me. I moved my nose toward her and stretched on the floor. She followed me to the floor and ever-so gently touched me, stroking her tiny hand back and forth on my head. I don't think I ever had felt a gentler touch. Her smile grew, and she drew closer.

OK! I like her!

I rolled on to my back and showed her my belly. She rubbed it and giggled a little, looking back at her mama, who smiled and took a photo.

Another little girl, who seemed to have difficulty walking, came toward me with the help of her person. She touched my belly. And then, a little boy did the same.

All the big humans were smiling broadly and thanking Steve.

As we walked out of the swinging doors, Steve led me to a grassy area so I could look for doggie breaking news alerts.

"Roxie, you did a good thing with those children. You brought a smile to their faces and their mamas. And me."

One of Steve's t-shirts displays these words: *Dogs speak but only to those who know how to listen.*

Sounds simple to me. Why would anyone want to speak to someone who will not listen?

You know, when I think about it, I don't believe I do anything special. I sit. I look at the human speaking to me. I accept her kind touch. I don't growl at her. In fact, when I roll on my back, I'm showing her that I have no intention of doing harm.

Treat me well. I want to treat you better. I want to bring you joy. I am grateful when you listen to my needs, too.

Don't humans do the same sort of thing?

Beyond the Biscuit

I have found that the way a human first approaches me sets the tone for our meeting. If he is all up in my face waving his hands, touching me with a heavy hand, and yelling, I am not so interested in being in that human's space. Oh, I'll give the benefit of the doubt. But not for long.

How do you greet people? How do you like people to greet you?

WHEN STRANGERS BECOME FRIENDS

HOW DO DIFFERENCES OF APPEARANCE, SIZE, COLOR, AGE, GENDER, AND FAMILY BACKGROUND AFFECT HOW YOU MIX WITH PEOPLE?

I'm an only dog. That gives me, pretty much, Steve and Hoppi's full attention. When Steve and I go for walks, it's just us. At night during couch time, it's just the three of us. When Steve is tapping on those keys in his office, I can stretch out on my fluff pillow. The same for my crates. They are my own one-bed apartment. I am not food insecure. My bowl, with satisfying food, is in the same place every day. And the biscuits. Well, you already know about the biscuits.

And while being the only dog has its perks, it does have a few drawbacks. You see, I'm what you might call a social animal. I love to meet new beings. They intrigue me. Anytime Steve and I encounter another dog and her person in the park or on the beach, I like to stop, sit, and watch. Steve says I am vigilant. I don't know about that. I am curious, and I feed off interaction.

In an earlier story, I told you about the little yellow building. What is so great about that place is that I get a chance to sniff, run, jump, and play with lots of dogs. Some bigger than me; others smaller. And we have fun. All day. All the time. Even when I get to sleep in the yellow building at night, I take in all the smells and scents of my buddies in the crates all around me. Occasionally, we will *doggie talk* to one another before we all close our eyes for the night. One large sleepover.

One day, some friends of Steve and Hoppi came to our home for a visit. While visits are not unusual, this time the humans brought their dog, Bear. He stands several paws taller than me, has long soft, golden hair. And he always smiles. I've come to understand that is how all Golden Retrievers are. Happy looking. At least those that I have met.

I've noticed when humans meet for the first time, there seems to be an awkward moment. They don't seem comfortable. Like they fear one another. Now, I've never seen a fight or anything like that. They remind me of those first times Steve introduced me to the steps at our home. I just sat there, unable to move. Newly introduced humans usually stand facing each other. They might shake hands, but I have never seen anyone of them sniff or rub up against another human. They seem a bit uptight.

Not Bear and me. Steve and Bear's person, Jeanne, introduced us at the backyard gate of our home. We were both on leash.

"Bear, sit."

"Roxie, sit."

We were about ten or fifteen paw prints away from each other. And then *click!* Both Jeanne and Steve unsnapped our leashes. But Bear and I remained seated as we had not been given a release command.

As soon as Steve and Jeanne said, "OK!" we were off. Running around the back yard. Of course, Bear had to first stop and mark his spot.

Wow, he is big and strong. Just look at how he balances on three legs. Impressive.

I didn't mind because, well, it was obviously my yard. He was just leaving a scent so that I would remember him when he went home. I could feel our friendship beginning.

As we continued to run and occasionally stop to do the play bow in front of each other, Steve and Jeanne remained with us, like chaperones at a dance. Eventually, I led Bear inside and up the stairs.

See, you may be big, but I'm not afraid of these stairs. Watch how fast I can run up to the next floor!

I shared my water with Bear. I would have shared my food, but his humans brought some for him. He did find one of my fuzzy bouncy balls and began showing off a bit. Rolling on his back and using the ball to massage his gums.

We both felt right at home with one another. Later we walked to the beach and went in the water. That tested me a bit. Since Bear is taller, he was able to go a bit further than me. But I didn't let him see fear in my eyes. Actually, he stretched me to go a little further than I ever had before.

Bear was respectful. He never entered any of my crates. I would not have minded; he was my new friend, after all. But he was content to lie on the floor.

We slept in different rooms that night, as it should be. After all, we had just met.

When we got up in the morning, we said hello with our play bows. We played with the ball. First him getting it and me chasing. Then me taking it, and him coming to me.

We never barked or snapped at one another. There was no biting. We played nicely. I know I was able to be myself with Bear and hope he was with me. I think some of that had to do with our work with Steve and Jeanne. I found out, we were both pet therapy dogs. Bear visited children who did not feel well, and he and Jeanne went to a building where people had to go when they were accused of misbehaving. We both had a purpose to be proud of.

When he left with his humans later that morning, I walked him to the car and watched him jump in the backseat.

Bear entered our house as a stranger and left as a friend.

Beyond the Biscuit

Meeting someone for the first time creates a sense of vigilance. That's a word Steve uses for me a lot. He says I'm vigilant. Well, I like to think of myself as observant. I look at who is in front of me and their actions. I wait for the proper time to greet. And I want to say hello to everyone. Whether sitting or play bowing, I let the other being know that I want to say hello. I want to find out about them. I have seen some dogs attempt to exert their top dog mentality by growling or lunging with bared teeth.

How rude.

When you first meet someone, how do you react? Do you get to know them, or do you begin to tell them all about you? What is your version of a play bow? Bear and I have differences: breed, shape, size, color, and family background. That does not matter to us. Does it matter when you meet someone?

CATS

WHAT HAVE YOU FOUND HELPFUL
TO START CONVERSATIONS?

I don't get cats.

I want to, and not in the way you might be thinking. I don't want to hurt them, just get to know them. I want to do the doggie handshake with them. No matter what I do, they remain aloof. I think I might be pushing a little too hard, and it is embarrassing. Here's how our meetings typically go.

Steve and I will be walking down the street when I spy one of the fleeting felines. I'll stop, my ears perked, and stare at them. And then—and this is difficult for me to admit—I start to whimper a little. I know, I know. It's pitiful.

Mhmhmh. Mhmhmh. Mhmhmh.

"Roxie, sit." Steve closely watches me as I pull a bit on the leash attempting to get closer to the cat.

What do the cats do? Usually, they sit there and then start cleaning themselves. Not even an acknowledgement! What's wrong with them? I start to think it might be me. All I want to do is get close. Geez, you'd think curiosity will kill the cat or something.

One day I did get close. I mean nose-to-belly close. We had just walked through the park and were on our street heading home.

As usual, I was in the grass reading the paper for breaking alerts when I stopped and began my undignified cat-sighting ritual.

"Hello, Malfred," Steve said. And then, stepping between me and the cat, he reached down and stroked the cat's black fur. The cat rubbed up against him. And all I heard was a contented sound from the little guy.

Purr. Purr. Purr.

For whatever reason, Steve knows these cats. *He* can be friends. But not *me*!

But on this day, Malfred remained stretched out on the ground as Steve gently inched me closer. And I mean *inched.* We would walk a step, and then I'd have to sit. Then another step and another sit. And so on. Malfred rolled to his back and showed his belly.

Hey! That's my move.

Steve was being very careful that I would not get too excited and scare Malfred. Finally—I mean *FINALLY!*—I was able to sniff the cat. For about three seconds. Then Malfred got up and moved about a paw length away, sat down, with his back to me, and began licking himself again.

That was it. He then walked away. Did not inquire about me. No kitty handshake. Nothing.

Mhmhmh. Mhmhmh. Mhmhmh.

What do I have to do to get close, make friends, and play?

I don't get cats.

Beyond the Biscuit

Have you ever had difficulty striking up a conversation or developing a relationship with someone you would like to know? Maybe it's a neighbor, like Malfred. Or maybe it's someone where you work or play.

What have you found helpful to start a conversation with another being who seems cool to you? Should you just walk away? Steve reminds me, it's not about me. It's about Malfred. Malfred is being Malfred. I shouldn't push it he says. But I think it is a lost opportunity not to develop a connection with a neighbor.

What do you think? What would you do if you were in my paws?

REPEAT. REPEAT. REPEAT, AGAIN.

HOW HAS DISCIPLINE BENEFITED YOU? IN WHAT AREAS OF YOUR LIFE DO YOU NEED A BIT MORE DISCIPLINE?

I often hear humans say to Steve, "What a well-behaved dog she is!" Like they expected me to be jumping up, down, and sideways while barking and carrying on. When I sit beside Steve, I am amazed how many humans think such a simple task is such a big deal.

But then, when I look around at some other dogs and their people, I can see from whence their surprise emanates. (Did you notice my vocabulary in the last sentence? I've been practicing!)

Don't get me wrong. I can pull at the leash a little harder than I should. Or get focused on something and tune Steve out. But, generally, I know what I need to do. And I do it. Not because I'm a genius dog like I hear the Doodle dogs are. No, the discipline comes from constant rehearsal led by maestro Steve.

Do you remember when I told about the two classes Steve and I participated in when I was a younger pup? Well, Steve won't forget them! Ever. He reminds me of our training. Always.

Like when I decide to pull at the leash and move directly to the side of the road where I know I can find important news alerts in the grass. If you were watching, you would see something like this.

Oh! Over there on that grass. I can smell that Baby was here. Gotta check it out.

"Roxie, no," Steve says and corrects my errant move to the left.

OK. But, really, I need to see if Baby is OK. So, let me go for a quick sniff.

"Roxie, watch me."

OK. But after I check it out.

"Roxie!"

At this point, Steve will stop walking and call me to his side. I sit with my ears back hoping my pitiful look will bring mercy. Not likely, as I know the routine to follow.

"Roxie, sit." Then we move about 5 steps forward before Steve makes an about face to the left and we are walking back to where we started. But we are not finished. We then make an about face to the right and walk a few steps. He stops. I sit.

At that point, he always leans into my snout, smiles, and, while gently rubbing my chest reminds me, "Roxie, watch me." I then get a sliver of a biscuit. And we continue our walk with me at his side.

Steve does not yell at me for these indiscretions, though I know by the tone of his voice that he does get a bit bothered. He does not spank me. He repeats the routines we learned long ago, so I do not forget them.

One day, our practice paid off big time.

It was the first day we were on duty at the place people *come to go*. One of the things we have to do there is stand in a line where Steve empties his pockets before we walk through what looks like a doorway without a door. There is a uniformed human on the other side, and he or she waves us through. First me, Steve holding the leash; and then Steve follows.

Well, on that first day, as I walked through some kind of bell beeped or a light went off or something happened, because the human stopped me.

Oh, no.

I sat there, ears back. I admit, I was a bit scared. You see there were lots of people with bags on wheels, lots of noise, and lots of movement. Now, I didn't freak out or anything uncool like that. But I was a bit concerned. I looked back at Steve who had not come through the door yet.

Yo! A little help, please!

"You'll have to remove her collar and leash," said the unsmiling human standing there. "The metal set of the alarm."

So, I went back to Steve. He did as instructed.

"Now, you come through first, and the dog can come next."

"Roxie," Steve leaned into me with a soft yet serious voice. "Stay!" And with that he put his hand out in stop motion. I knew he meant business from our training. He turned his back and walked through the doorway.

I sat there. Unleashed. Commotion all around me. I focused on Steve.

"Now, the dog can come through," said the person who had just waved Steve through.

Steve got down to his knee and looked at me. "Roxie. OK, come!"

I did. He loved on me. We must have passed because we got our stuff from the moving table and went to work. I am glad we had practiced the *stay*, *sit* and, *come* routines. I think that probably saved my biscuits that day.

Oh, and later that day, Steve bought a new leash for me so that it would not set off the alarms. He is a quick study, I must say.

Beyond the Biscuit

When and how has "repeat, repeat, and repeat again" helped you be a better person or do something with more skill? What do you need to devote more practice time to at this point in your life? When will you start?

LEARNING TO LET GO

I LEARNED EARLY ON THAT THERE WAS NO NEED TO GET WOUND UP AND CHASE MY TAIL ABOUT THINGS I HAVE NO CONTROL OVER. HOW ABOUT YOU?

I hear Steve tell other humans, "I hit the jackpot with Roxie. She's so calm and easy to work with."

And, I guess, he is correct. Not sure about "the jackpot" part, but I do know that I am pretty mellow. Not remembering my mother, or ever knowing my father, I cannot speak for my background.

I think I just learned early on that there was no need to get wound up and chase my tail about things I have no control over. Just makes dog sense to me. As I've said before, I am about economy of motion.

Maybe it is the fact that even though I had been abandoned beside that road long ago, I *was* rescued. Perhaps it is because I realize my needs *will be* met by caring humans. Other than the aforementioned people on top of the boards on top of the wheels, I am pretty easy going.

Truth be told, though, there was one other thing that made my short hair stand on end for a brief while. It was when I was still a young pup, and we would walk through the park. I'm embarrassed to even mention it, but, after all, this is a memoir of sorts. So, I'll fess up.

Turtles. Yep, those goofy looking creatures who hang alongside the park pond. For whatever reason, I went into a frenzy every time I saw them. Close to the same reaction as when I saw those people on top of the boards on top of the wheels. Not sure why. Steve worked with me. Biscuits, of course, were used to help me control my emotions. And, eventually, me and those turtles learned to co-exist. I look at them now and wonder whatever drove me to distraction. Guess it was just a puppy stage thing I was going through

There, I feel better now.

I've already mentioned that we have a frequent ritual that I have grown to anticipate and enjoy. At first, I was a bit anxious but the way Steve introduced me to this practice helped me let go of my fears. He is methodical and predictable, and I guess I have found that comforting.

The first sign of what is to come are the towels. Steve will place them in the room where he and Hoppi wash their bodies. He then opens a glass door into a space where water comes out of the wall. And, of course, I do what I think any thoughtful dog would do. I walk in and sit down. Steve joins me. Turns on the water, and he gets me all soaped up. The water is warm. He is always careful to keep water from getting into my eyes. What I like the best is that I get a rub down. It is relaxing and feels so good. Almost as good as biscuits. Almost.

When the weather is warm, we do the same routine outside with a hose that comes from the house wall.

After he rinses the soapy foam from my body, he dries me with the towels. The brisk rub down feels good. Steve puts towels on the floor, and I lower my head and move my snout around. Then I lean into them with my side. First one, then the other, followed by rolling on my back and wiggling back and forth. Invigorating!

One other thing I like about this water ritual. Whatever he uses on my fur, it does not stink. I feel good—like a dog. There have been times when Steve has sprayed my crate or the rug in his office with smelly spray stuff. He must like it, but it is not very *doggy*, if you get my drift. It kind of fouls up the scent of being a dog. I like to smell real smells that all the perfume stuff gets in the way of. Steve is learning to respect that. I think that is a reason I don't fuss with the water and soap. I know it's going to happen, and he knows what he's doing. He respects my needs. I let go and trust.

I learned that soon after the bath, Steve and I get in the car and visit people in either buildings where they *come to stay* or *come to go*. The bath became a signal that I would be meeting lots of people who would smile, talk, and rub my fur. A win-win situation.

Beyond the Biscuit

Control. Is control a big thing for you? That is, do you spend time and energy attempting to control everything that you encounter? How does this make you feel? Do you have someone like Steve who can help you get through times that make you anxious? Like when I first came to know the turtles.

What represents the turtles in your life? That is, what makes your fur stand on end, when, in reality, there is no need to be frenzied? Who can help you? Who has helped? What were your biscuits in those times? That is, what served as incentives and re-inforcers for you?

I hear humans say that their dogs hate baths. Not sure why. I think Steve has made them something I look forward to rather than fear. Can you think of something you now do, that at one time filled you with anxiety? How did you move beyond panic to accep-tance? Who helped you? What advice would you have for someone who is attempting to confront a situation that brings on the jitters and maybe even panic?

A FEW THOUGHTS ABOUT COSTUMES AND MISCALCULATIONS

HAVE YOU EVER MADE AN ERROR IN JUDGMENT AND EMBARRASSED SOMEONE?

For two beings who do not speak the same oral language, Steve and I have come to know each other's needs, non-verbal cues, and odd little quirks.

For instance, when Steve calls me to come in the house from the patio, often I will lie there and stare at him.

"Come, Roxie."

I look at him.

"Come, Roxie."

I lick my paw.

"Roxie, come!"

Like changing the order of words will do anything.

Then Steve will look at me and say, "Roxie, sit." Sometimes he does not say the words but gives me the sit request with his hand. (Note: I often ignore *commands*; but I will entertain *requests*.)

I sit.

"Stay."

I stare intently at Steve.

"OK! Come!"

And I bound in the house. Not sure why. But that order of signals works for me.

Another human habit of his involves a board he lies on in the Garnasium. He straps his feet in at the base, and then tips himself upside down! I know, sounds strange. While lying on this board, his feet are in the air and his head toward the floor. I help by coming along and licking his face. That's just how I am.

We are, I think the word is, simpatico. (Impressed?)

Except one day when Steve just was not thinking.

We met up with a few other dogs and their people at the building where people *come to stay*. I had met most of the dogs before, so nothing new there.

But each dog, including me, had on a ridiculous outfit. I mean ludicrous, shameful, undignified. I can't speak for the other dogs. They swore me to secrecy. So, I will just speak for myself.

I heard all of the humans talking about *Halloween*. It appears, that on this day, humans make believe they are someone or something else. I guess they get to fantasize for a few hours. Some make their noses longer and their hair black. Others have glitter and sparkles on their bodies and in their hair. I don't get it. But if it makes them happy, so be it.

Unfortunately, we canines were made to participate in this demeaning exercise. I like how I look just fine. But, for whatever reason, Steve wrapped my body in this red, white, and blue *thing*. I only know it was red white, and blue because I kept hearing, "Roxie looks so good in red, white, and blue."

Really? I will gladly give it to you, m' lady if you like it so much!

A few people referred to me as Wonder Woman. Steve even tied a thing to my head that kept falling off.

Everyone was looking and giggling at the dog outfits. They were so proud and happy.

It was bad enough to be in public around other dogs like this, but Steve decided we needed to walk around the building and visit people.

Really?

Besides the indignity, this monstrosity did not fit me well. Every step I took, the hideous thing would either shift, bind, or slide. We'd stop, and Steve would readjust and tighten or loosen. Nothing ever worked.

Finally, when it was obvious Steve was not thinking clearly, I just stopped. Dead. In. My. Tracks.

"What's the matter, Roxie? Need me to readjust?"

Nope. Need you to gain your usual good senses.

I stretched out on the cool tile floor, attempting to blend in with my surroundings.

"Come, Roxie."

Ain't happening.

Then he went through the hand signals and the sit, stay, come routine.

Nope. Not moving. Get this thing off of me.

Finally, he took the hideous outfit off of me. I looked at him and shook my head.

What were you thinking?

I got a biscuit, and we went to visit my people.

Sometimes, a dog just has to stand her ground and let her feelings be known.

Beyond the Biscuit

Steve meant well that day. He was in the spirit and thought I would be, too. He miscalculated.

Have you ever done that with someone? Made an error in judgment, perhaps embarrassing that person? You did not mean to, but you did. How did you handle the situation? What lessons did you gain moving forward?

When it comes to purpose, we have to remember why we do things and why we ask others to do things. Are we clear with our intent? Have we given the others involved the opportunity to speak and voice their opinions?

DOGONAL

HOW DO YOU STAY TRUE TO YOUR LIFE AND NOT LIVE ACCORDING TO THE OPINIONS OF OTHERS?

I made up a word. It's a good word. A very good word. More dogs might want to consider it,

IMHCO (In My Humble Canine Opinion).

Dogonal.

Repeat after me.

Dog-o-nal.

Admittedly, listening to humans inspired my vocabulary intervention. I've heard them say that so and so should not take things so gosh darn *personal.* That they should go with the flow and understand that when someone barks at you, it is usually more about them than it is you.

Canines have their ego issues just like humans. They have to strut their top dog stuff around. Some, as I have witnessed from afar, will attack and harm another dog. From my vantage point, they lack social skills and pup-esteem.

So, they lash out for no one's good.

I will stop and look at them.

Do you need to woof? Would you like to play bow? Having a tough day? Do you need alone time? OK, we can play at another time when you feel better.

If you really think about it, dogs could easily get their tails out of joint with their humans. How would you feel if every day you got the same food in the same dish beside the same water bowl in the same place? Or, if every time you went somewhere with a friend, that person slid a collar around your neck and led you where he wanted to go? Or made you walk on very hot pavement in your bare paws? Not a comfortable picture, is it?

I have been fortunate to meet dogs who model the-nothing-*dogonal* model. Especially if they have caring and compassionate humans in their lives.

I would rather live by the rule to take nothing *dogonal* than to bark, growl, and snap. When a dog barks and shows his teeth at me, that does not make me a lesser pup. In fact, Steve and I usually just acknowledge the yapper and walk away.

"Good girl, Roxie. You never seem to take anything *personal*. I could learn a lot from you."

Dogonal, that is. And yes, you could.

Beyond the Biscuit

Admittedly, it can be difficult to walk away from an insult or slight, perceived or real. What suggestions do you have to live *your* life, not one based on what *others* yell at you? How do you remember that someone's opinion of you does not necessarily reflect who you are?

KNOT AT THE END OF THE ROPE

WHAT OR WHO HELPS (OR HAS HELPED) YOU HANG ON WHEN THINGS GET TOUGH?

At times, we learn lessons when we least expect them. For instance, I learned how to gain a bit of control from one of the toys in my crate. While I don't play with them much, I do have toys. Over the years, Steve has surprised me with one in my crate every so often. He's that way.

When I first arrived from the building that had all the puppy crates, I had a few hard objects to chew. I really liked to gnaw on these. They helped me pass time as I could chew, and chew, and they never seemed to get smaller. A challenge. But one day they disappeared.

"The vet said these could hurt your teeth, Roxie. Here's a soft toy to play with."

Whatever.

When I visited the building with all those little people with little hands and loud little voices, they gave me a gift for stopping by. A stuffed toy shaped like, they said, a skunk. I'm not sure what a skunk is but it was cute. When I chomped down on it, the skunk talked to me.

"*Squeak!*"

Another toy looks like a duck. This one also talks but, I have to admit, the first few times it spoke to me I just tilted my head in disbelief.

"*Quack. Quack! Quaaaaaaaaaaaaaaaaaack!*"

A bit odd, but it has grown on me.

At times, when I have lots of energy, I will move my toys, one at a time, from one room to another. I pick them up and zoom into Steve's office. I drop the toy and then drop into a play bow right in front of it. Of course, it never responds, so I run to fetch another toy and zoom back to the office. And I repeat until all the toys are scattered along the floor. I then sit back and look at my collection. Proud. Kind of like herding toys.

One day, Steve seemed to be a bit upset about something. He was at his desk, tapping away at those keys with his fingers. He was talking to himself. Unbeknownst (like that word?) to him, I had quietly gathered and lined up all the toys behind his chair. When he turned around, that serious look on his face melted to a smile as he looked at the stuffed creatures staring up at him.

"You are a doodle, Roxie." And he scratched my ears. "Let's get you some food."

Yum!

One of the toys goes with me when I stay overnight at the little yellow building. It is simple. Steve is a fan—a big fan—of keeping things as simple as possible. This toy is a rope with a knot tied at each end. No squeak. No talk. Just rope. Nice.

Steve will pick up the rope and attempt to get me to pull on it with him. Kind of like a tug of war. I'm not much of a fan, but, occasionally, I indulge Steve. It makes him happy.

When I do tug back, I place my front legs straight out, raise my haunches up and pull with little backward sliding movements. This is where the knots come in handy. As Steve pulls, the rope will slip bit by bit from my jaws. But when I reach that knot, I get a better grip and dig in with all my might. I feel more in control. I feel strong!

All because of a knot at the end of my rope.

This helps me gather myself and then keep moving toward my goal of wresting the rope from Steve.

The knot at the end of my rope.

Everyone could use one.

Beyond the Biscuit

Have you ever felt like something or someone was slipping away from you? You want to hold on, but you feel like you just cannot hang on any longer. You needed help.

What or who helps (or has helped) you tie a knot at the end of your rope to keep you hanging on when the going gets tough? How have you helped someone by being a knot at the end of her or his rope?

NICE TO MEET YOU, I THINK.

WHAT RULES OF CIVILITY DO YOU FOLLOW WHEN YOU GREET PEOPLE?

We need to talk. I know you humans mean well, but that doesn't make this any easier. Specifically, I need to woof about how you decide to greet me and my pup friends.

I see how you say "hi" to one another as I walk with Steve. Sometimes, it might be a wave of the hand and a "How ya doing?" greeting as you pass one another. Nice. Cordial. Polite.

Other times, people will come right up to Steve, talking loudly, and patting Steve on the back. Some people like to hug. Steve rolls with it. Truth be told, he can be loud. And he is a hugger, too. He means well.

What I have never seen, though, is one person run up to Steve, put her arm out in front of Steve's face, and then rub his nose and hair and scratch his ears.

Never!

So, why do you do that to me? Don't get me wrong. I am glad you want to be friends and show me the love. I do, too. But give me a little space.

I have watched and listened to Steve when he talks with little people who want to meet me for the first time. First, he has me sit beside him. If the little person appears to be rushing at me, Steve will step in front of me, smile and talk softly.

"This is Roxie. I am glad you want to meet her. Can you help with something before you say hello?"

The little person looks up at Steve as he kneels to the floor with one hand on my back.

"I want you to think about how you and I just met. What would you have thought if I ran up to you, my hand waving toward your face, speaking loudly, and then touching your head, ears, and hair? Might be a little scary."

Steve, still smiling, suggests that the little person wait for the dog's person to extend an invitation to touch the dog.

"And, when you get that permission, slowly extend your hand below Roxie's chin. Let her sniff you. Let her get used to you."

This usually leads to a very soft stroke under my chin. Steve watches every move and never leaves my side. I relax and assume my favorite position—I roll over on my back and expose my belly.

This is so much better than the person who decides that I immediately need my view obscured by his hands and my body enveloped in a bear hug of sorts.

Excuse me! We have just met. A little courtesy, please. How would you like it if I just barrel right into your midsection and root around there? I didn't think you would!

I want to meet you. Steve wants you to meet me. Let's follow a few rules of civility for everyone's comfort level. Once we know each other, then we can play.

Beyond the Biscuit

When you first meet someone, how do you greet that person? Are you loud? Do you get right up in her face? How does the person react? How do you like to be greeted? Why do you think this is an important lesson for humans to understand—about dogs and their fellow humans?

NICKNAMES

WHAT LITTLE QUIRKS AND PERSONALITY TRAITS MAKE YOU WHO YOU ARE?

I thought Steve had lost his senses. Maybe it was too much time tapping on those keys in his office.

"Are you ready, *Freddy?*

Huh?

He stood at the bottom of the stairs, leash in his hands. "Are you ready *Freddy?*" he said again with a smile on his face.

Who on earth is Freddy?

But since I saw the leash, I knew that meant a walk—which eventually led to a biscuit. I thought maybe I'd see this Freddy at some point. I never did.

Then I caught on. It appears Steve was just having fun with me. You know, kind of joking around by calling me *Freddy;* making a rhyme. Odd, but OK with me. I grew to understand when he used that word, what it meant.

I've mentioned in previous stories how Steve likes to call me a wack-a-doodle. Most people laugh when they hear him say that (except some of those who have *real* Doodle dogs. They tend to scrunch up their faces. Not sure they are amused.)

Usually, I get wack-a-doodle, or *doodle* for short, when I do something he finds funny or idiosyncratic. (Like that word? I've been studying an ACT/SAT word prep game with Steve and Hoppi. I'm a quick study. But he hasn't called me Brainiac yet.)

"You're such a *doodle*, Roxie." I wag my tail.

I make no excuses about the naps I like to take. They keep me fresh. And, I don't need a crate or fluff pillow to indulge. I've been known to just lay down wherever and doze. Like when we are walking and Steve stops to speak with other humans. I sit for a while. Then, as they continue to yammer, I lie down. And then go into a full stretch and close my eyes. At times, I even roll on my back, legs in the air, and belly exposed to the sky. Right there in the street. Very comfortable and cool. If they are going to stand there and talk, I'm going to be comfortable.

Steve will look down at me and say, "You're a doodle!"

Whatever.

When I nap around the house, Steve will check on me, scratch my ears and call me *Lazy Bones*. I think he might be jealous because I take breaks. I am doing my best to rub off on him.

One day as we made our rounds at the place that people *come to stay*, a man in a white coat walked by us. He looked official and important. I heard someone say, "Good morning, doctor."

The doctor smiled when he saw me, and Steve introduced us. "This is Roxie. We are part of the hospital's pet therapy program."

The doctor gave me a nod. One of the nurses made an *aww* sound.

"Everyone knows Roxie; no one knows this old guy with her." The doctor smiled and said, "That's because Roxie is a *ROX STAR*."

Steve laughed. And from that day on more people referred to me as the *Rox Star*. I kind of like it.

One of the best names I like is when Steve calls me *Little Girl*. "*Little Girl* is in the backyard." Or "Where is *Little Girl?*" Or "Hey *Little Girl*, want to go for a walk?" I like being his *Little Girl*.

I have grown to like all these names as they represent a piece of who I am. Steve has taken time to understand my little quirks. Rather than make fun of me or yell at me, he has accepted them and me. By doing so, he acknowledges and respects me for who I am.

Beyond the Biscuit

Before I toss a few questions your way, I want to pause and address *labels* for a moment. Someone who does not know Steve and me might think the names (the labels) he places on me are insulting or demeaning. Steve and I know they are not; we understand one another. And when you consider that his actions are always respectful and loving, the labels take on a special meaning.

You might want to consider that before labelling others. Do they understand the labels and why you use them? Do you know why you are using them? Have you taken care to make sure the labels do not offend or hurt people? Be mindful of how you address and speak to and about others.

Steve's labels have come from him paying attention to me, what I do, and how I do it. What are some of your little quirks and personality traits that make you who you are? How have these come to define you and influence your interaction with other people?

PEOPLE BISCUITS

WHAT ROUTINES DISTRACT YOU FROM YOUR PURPOSE?

I have come to learn that humans have their own form of biscuits. And most carry them wherever they go. They do not seem to leave them be for very long. In fact, it looks like they are led by these things. Like fish chasing the bait of fishermen from the beach. They can't help themselves.

My biscuits come in the shape of small bones. Emphasis on *small*. Steve knows I would eat my weight in biscuits if left to my own devices, so he moderates the size. And he seems to know the right time for biscuit delivery.

The humans' call their biscuits *phones*. They must have a strong attraction—more than my biscuits do for me—because they cannot seem to be without them. And when they have them (which is always), they seem to look at them more than the people they are with. I know, seems odd to me, too.

Some humans carry them in their pockets. Others hold on to them at all times, no matter what. I even saw one young woman get up from her beach chair to go for a swim. She walked into the water with the phone in her hand. Can you say *oblivious*? (I can because I continue to build my vocabulary.) She got her feet wet, and then noticed her hand, returned to the chair, and placed the phone on her towel.

When I'm with Steve, the only time he pulls the phone from his pocket is to point it at the ocean.

"That is a great picture, Roxie. Beautiful sunrise!"

Sometimes he calls to me. "Roxie, look. Look here. Smile for the camera! "

I'm not much for taking *doggies*. It interrupts my connection to the smells and sounds around me. There's pee-mail out there for me to sniff.

The phones do seem to have a strange attraction for the humans. Almost like the phone is saying, "Follow me. Look at me. Listen to me."

Maybe they provide a human form of pee-mail. Something so strong that they are unable to focus on anything else.

Steve moderates my biscuits. That has trained me to focus on what is around me rather than a single-minded attention to something that can control me rather than me control my own life.

There might be a lesson in that for other beings.

Beyond the Biscuit

We all have routines of sort. Some keep us in shape. Others keep us sharp and focused. And some can become distracting if we allow them to be.

Do you have a phone that you constantly follow like I follow my nose to the ground? Has it come to be a distraction, always at your reach or firmly in your hand? Maybe you were one of those people I have seen on the beach who, while walking with a friend, never looks at that person or the ocean or the sea shells, but rather keeps looking at the phone. Why do people do that? Why do you do it— or if you do not, why not? Have you ever attempted to moderate your phone use? How did that go? What is your next step?

ANXIOUS PERSON, ANXIOUS PET

HOW DOES THE COMPANY YOU KEEP IMPACT HOW YOU FEEL AND ACT?

Have you ever noticed how dogs seem to mirror the humans they hang with? Take Baby for instance. Her person, Bob, always greets me with a friendly hello and then rubs my back, head, haunches, and shoulders. Kind of like a full-body massage. Nice. Very nice.

Baby jumps with me as we both do the doggie handshake. We rub against each other, sniff, and then sit waiting for the biscuits we know Steve has buried in his pocket.

Baby has never growled at me. Never ignored me. (Though, at times, if the cat is nearby, she might postpone our doggie handshake.) Bob has never growled at Steve. Never ignored him. Bob and Baby make a nice couple, and they make good friends.

When we approach other dogs and their people, Steve is respectful of their space. He will always look at me and say, "Watch me, Roxie. Watch me." As we get closer, he reminds me, "Leave it, Roxie. Leave it."

Those are my cues to focus on Steve's words and not go acting nutso by jumping and lunging. At times, we will stop, and I will sit watching the approaching dog. I cannot tell you how many times the other person has said, while looking at me, "What a good dog! I wish my fur baby acted like that."

If I could speak human, I would tell them about all the work we have been through and still do.

Hey, this good-looking pup in front of you took a lot of practice to get like this. Now, by chance, do you have a biscuit?

One day as we approached a dog and its person on the beach, Steve said hello like he always does. This person barely acknowledged us. She looked frightful. Eyes wide open as if she expected a fish to jump out of the water and gobble up her little ankle biter, who also appeared to be nervous and anxious. Nothing like Bob and Baby.

I am not sure what comes first. The anxious and wide-eyed people or the jumpy canines with them?

As for me and my person, I think we have rubbed off on one another. I think I have helped him to chill a bit.

Beyond the Biscuit

Do you think people can influence how their dogs react to the world? That is, if a dog has a nervous person, do you think that nervousness can be transferred to the dog? How about the other way around— can a dog transfer feelings and behavior to its person?

How about human to human? Does the company you keep have an impact on how you feel and act? If it does, how do you pick the right people with whom to be friends?

LITTLE THINGS ADD UP TO BIG THINGS

WHAT SMALL ACTION DO YOU OR CAN YOU DO TO HELP A PERSON SMILE, RELAX, OR JUST BREATHE A BIT EASIER?

One of my blog followers reminded me of the importance of having someone in your corner. A human, canine, or other being nearby for support.

At the end of one of my posts, I asked if the readers had ever felt alone or lost, and if they had, who was there for them. One reader wrote,

> *...when I've needed some help finding my way now and then, my wonderful Dad has been there as a role model, supporter, cheerleader and mentor. I'm so grateful to have such a wonderful father, just like you must be to have such wonderful humans!*

That reminded me how fortunate I have been. From the person who found me on the side of that road at the beginning of my story to my "Gotcha Day" to where I sit today, I have had more cheer-leaders than I can count on my paws and dewclaws.

No doubt about it, I am a lucky pup. There are pups out there who struggle because no one is on their side or in their crate, if you know what I mean.

Sometimes we might forget about the little things in life that add up to big things. You see, ever since way back in that puppy room I've always had enough food to eat and water to drink. When I hear the rain and thunder outside, I don't have to worry about getting wet. And at those times when I just need *me time*, I have crates, fluff pillows, and stuffed toys.

And then there are Steve and Hoppi. Their mere presence is comfort for me. Every morning, Hoppi places a blanket out for me to sit (well, really, stretch out) next to her while she sits, sips, and scans. Steve is like clockwork when it comes to our walks to the beach and around the park. And the baths and showers are plentiful.

Since I cannot speak human language and say thank you, I have come to rely on my body language. Like when Steve is at his desk and tapping on those keys, I will curl up under his desk and snuggle up to his feet. It's my way of saying, *Even when you work, I want to be with you.*

There are times he gets a little upset (ok, a lot upset) with something (not me, of course). I can tell because his voice gets loud. He might start banging a little harder on those keys. I get his attention by placing my head on his leg and looking up at him. He *always* pauses and smiles at me. Kind of my biscuit for him.

And of course, there is our early morning nose nuzzle when Steve opens my crate door, and says, "Good morning, Roxie." I burrow into his legs rubbing my nose back and forth. He laughs and says, "Nose nuzzle. Nose nuzzle!" It's a little thing that makes me feel good and secure. And it brings a smile to his face. It's my way of starting the day with a cheer for Steve. And a thank you.

Thank you for the little things that you do that add up to the big things that add up to a life well-lived.

Beyond the Biscuit

I believe we all can do those little things that can make a difference in another being's life. That is why I do my best to greet any living being with a wag of my tail, a playful bow, and positive energy. It makes me feel good. And I hope it makes a difference for them as well.

Never underestimate the little things that build to bigger things that help make a life well-lived.

So, here is my question for you: What small action do you or can you do to help a person smile, relax, or just breathe a bit easier? And, a bonus question: How does this make you feel?

NON-INTERRUPTUS

HOW LONG CAN YOU SIT IN A GROUP AND MODEL NON-INTERRUPTUS BEHAVIOR?

I'll keep this short. Some humans and canines talk and woof too much. They don't know when to just be and let those around them speak.

You've seen it I'm sure. Like the humans who cannot *not* talk. I have been with Steve when he says something like, "Good morning! How are you today?"

Ten minutes later we are still there listening to her yammer on about whatever. Steve stands there listening. I usually roll over, close my eyes, and surrender.

How can one person talk so much about herself? And when will she pause to take a breath?

What's kind of odd is that humans like this very seldom ask Steve any questions. They just talk. And if Steve where to say something, they interrupt. And keep talking about themselves. Ad nauseum! (See, still building my word base. Practice.)

Canines do the same thing. You've heard them. You walk past them on the street and all they do is make noise.

Yelp! Yelp! Groooowl! Groooowl! Yap! Yap!

My preference is to assume the position of non-interruptus. Respect you. Listen to you. Play with you (if I have been invited to play). And then back off.

When we meet, I will do my best to make sure our meeting is all about you. Not all about me.

Once we start the conversation, let's make sure it's a conversation.

Beyond the Biscuit

This week I have a challenge for you. When you are with someone or with a group, how much time do you spend listening to and looking at the human or humans with you? How much time do they do the same for you? Do they spend more time interrupting you and going on about their stories, or do they ask questions about you? And, likewise, do you ask respectful and authentic questions about those in front of you, or do you just interrupt them to tell them your story?

How long can you sit in a group and model non-interruptus behavior?

THE NEIGHBORS

WHAT HAVE YOU DONE TO GET TO KNOW YOUR NEIGHBORS?

I have a nice second-floor porch deck. Very nice. With a TV, fluff pillow, and ceiling fan. Oh, there are chairs and footrests for Steve and Hoppi, too. The deck overlooks the backyard. From the top of the stairs, I get to cast an eye over my fiefdom (see, still building my vocabulary) below.

Funny how things change as one gets older and more experienced. These are the same stairs Steve attempted to get me to climb when I first arrived here. They initially irritated me about as much as those twerking squirrels. But, over time, I have mastered them one step at a time. Now, I bound up those little platforms without a thought. However, I digress.

When I do sit on the top step and view the yard below, I can see my neighbors on one side of the house. Two canines live there. When they see me, they bark from their side of the fence. I sit and observe. I don't bark at them. Would like to get to know them a little better. While we have briefly met on the street, we haven't had a play day yet. Not sure why. But I'm guessing the humans have their reasons.

The house on the other side of my deck (err, Steve and Hoppi's deck) has two more dogs. They bark. A. Lot. I can see them when I am in my backyard and look up at their deck. They look down and bark. A. Lot. I hear them, also, when Steve and I walk by the front of their house. They jump up and down in front of their porch window and bark. A. Lot. When I am curled up on my deck fluff pillow, and they are inside their house, I can hear them bark. A. Lot.

I'm not sure if we will ever play.

Beyond the Biscuit

Why do you think some beings must bark. A. Lot? Do you ever attempt to get closer to these barking beings or do you keep your distance? Can the bark be a good thing—or should you be wary?

THE INSPIRATIONAL HATCHLING

WHY DO SOME BEINGS MOVE FORWARD IN SPITE OF WHAT SEEM TO BE OVERWHELMING ODDS, WHILE OTHERS SHRUG AND GIVE UP?

We were walking along the water's edge. My energy was pulling us forward. Every so often I'd turn back toward Steve and jump up and spin around, coming down with the leash in my mouth. Prancing and proud!

"You're a wack-a-doodle!" Steve laughed, and we continued toward our morning coffee.

As we passed a young woman walking in the opposite direction, Steve said hello and I wagged my tail. Then we heard the woman call out.

"Look! Oh, my God. It's a baby turtle."

We stopped, turned, and I saw it. The first time I had ever seen one that tiny. I see turtles every day in our park, but they are so much larger. This little critter was barely bigger than my paw. I immediately pulled Steve toward it.

"Whoa, Roxie, leave it!" Steve pulled me back. "You can't play with that little one. It's trying to get to the ocean."

I was beside myself. The little thing, all by itself on the sand, moving toward the ocean waves. That tiny creature heading for the huge ocean. What was it thinking? I wanted so badly to get closer and find out. I dropped to my belly, perked my ears, and attempted to inch closer. Steve shortened the leash.

And then I surprised myself with a sound that was the cross between a whimper, cry, and howl. I needed to be next to this little thing right now.

Steve got on his knees and held me and stroked my head and back.

"It's OK, Roxie. It's just trying to get to the water."

By now, a small crowd of humans huddled around. They kept using words like *hatchling, sea turtle, crawl,* and *alone.* All marveled at its determination.

"Poor thing got separated from the rest of the hatchlings somehow."

"Look how the waves keep pushing it back to shore."

"Can we pick it up and help it to the water?"

Steve continued stroking me as I focused on the little thing.

"Look at that," said one of the humans, "it looks like it's doing pushups."

The hatchling had just been pushed back by some water, and I could see it rising up and down on its tiny arms. Much like Steve does in the Garnasium, though, I confess, the turtle's form was a bit better. (Don't mention that to Steve. He does try hard.)

Then a young person walked up. She wore a blue shirt. Someone called her a *volunteer.* I saw her talking in one those things humans always carry in their hands. Then she kicked off her shoes, gently picked up the little turtle, and carried it into the ocean where she slowly placed it in the water and set it on its course.

I heard words like, *wow* and *inspiring* and *I sure hope the little thing survives.*

I was still in a state. I did not want to leave. When I did get up, I pulled Steve closer to the water.

Where are you little one? How did you do that? Why did you do that? You are all alone, and you still went into that big, huge rough water. Aren't you afraid?

I kept looking at the waves crashing on the sand. All the humans had departed to their lives. I stared at where I last saw the hatchling. I never had the chance to get really close for a sniff. Don't think it had a name. But it sure did inspire a lot of people.

Later that day, Steve shared the photo he took of the turtle. One of his friends said that one time she had seen a whole nest of these hatchlings make it to the sea. She told Steve, "They're so brave being so tiny but going straight into the ocean. It was a life-changing moment."

Odd, isn't it, something so small can have such a lasting impact on so many who appear to be so much larger. It did not let a force bigger than itself keep it from its goal. It did not quit.

A lesson taught. A lesson learned.

Beyond the Biscuit

It's not always about how big you are—or how big you are not. A great deal depends on your determination, motivation, desire, and discipline. The turtle on that day, no matter how many times it got pushed away from its goal, kept re-positioning itself, digging in, and moving forward.

Why do you think some beings are able to move forward in spite of what seem to be overwhelming odds? They never give up! While others surrender at the mere thought of an obstacle. In fact, they may never even start moving forward. They sit there defeated, never knowing what they could have been if they only stepped forward.

How do you keep going when the odds seem against you? What specific strategies do you use? Is there someone, like the little turtle, who inspires you to move when the going is difficult?

WE SETTLE IT OURSELVES

WHEN SOMEONE STEPS OUT OF BOUNDS, EITHER THROUGH WORDS OR ACTIONS, WHAT DO YOU FIND TO BE THE MOST APPROPRIATE WAY TO HANDLE IT?

Steve brought me to a new park in our beach neighborhood. It's one of those parks dedicated to us canines and appointed with cool accoutrements for the humans. (Like that one? Accoutrements! Steve continues to be a good influence on my vocabulary.)

We canines have lots of area to run at a full gallop. There are trees for shade and a patch of ground where water shoots up toward the sky for us to run through and cool off. Lots of water bowls, too.

The humans have seats, tables, and a long bar area with drinks and snacks. The humans can sit in the dog area or in the covered area behind the fence and watch us play.

As I do when we go to the little yellow building, I whimpered with excitement and anticipation as Steve parked the car. The sniffs and smells overwhelmed me. And when I saw all those dogs, well

I couldn't wait to get in and start running. And did I ever run! So much so that I quickly tired myself out.

"Roxie. Your tongue is longer than a politician's necktie," Steve said with a laugh.

I walked over to an area where a human tapped away on keys like Steve has in his office. (It seems to me that humans have a tough time leaving their work behind. They *really* need to follow a dog's lead from time to time. Stop and sniff the grass, if you know what I mean.) The ground was hard and cool. I sprawled out, huffing and puffing. Time for a rest.

Steve told me on the way home that, based on my panting and tongue length, I might need a little less couch time and more cardio time. While I enjoyed the visit, I fear I might be in for more exercise than I am used to, with Steve as my personal trainer.

Besides the physical activity and canine companionship, play yards like this offer a lesson for those willing to pay attention. You see, there must have been at least thirty dogs inside the play area. Big ones and tiny ones. Slow ones and fast ones. I had never met any of them before this visit, but we played like we had been buds for years. Occasionally, one dog would get a little nippy, yappy, or sappy. The others put up with it to a point. And then, one dog would take it on itself to stop and put that pup in his or her place. It's usually quick with no bloodshed or flaying paws. Just a quick, *Knock it off, Nimrod!* The offending dog often just rolls on its back, belly to the air, indicating he or she will not be a troublemaker any longer. And then everyone goes about their purpose for being in the yard.

No place for rudeness. And if there is, we settle it ourselves. No time to hold grudges. Clear communication amongst a pack of dogs from varying backgrounds. And then when that is over, we all do what we came to do. Play, exercise, and socialize.

Beyond the Biscuit

When someone steps out of bounds, either through words or actions, what do you find to be the most appropriate way to handle that? Us dogs will ignore it for a while, but if the behavior persists, we do something. We challenge the offending party. Like in the play yard. We settle the disagreement and move forward. No grudges. We want to be buds.

What do humans do?

COMFORTABLE IN MY FUR

IS YOUR CONVERSATION FILLED WITH A LOT OF
WOOFING ABOUT YOUR ACCOMPLISHMENTS, LIKES,
DISLIKES, AND DESIRES? OR DO YOU LISTEN—
REALLY LISTEN—TO THE BEING IN FRONT OF YOU?

One day, when we visited the dog park with the cool accoutrements, I helped Steve and Hoppi remember another important life lesson: Sometimes it is ok to sit in silence and observe others. Quiet can be a powerful tool to see—really see—how others behave and interact with the environment. It allows me to see who I would like to spend more time with and who I would just as rather leave be.

When I first meet another dog, I am excited, yet polite. I want to engage in the doggie handshake, but I am not interested in yapping and snapping. I'll do the doggie play bow and maybe even a play growl. We might run around the park a time or two. But then I'm good to lay down and watch the others for a while. I see dogs who have to run to the gate and bark at any new paws that enter. They have to jump, bump, and dump a whole lot of woofing about themselves.

Seems like a lot of energy. And then one dog tries to out woof the others until virtually no one is listening, and everyone is woofing. I sit to the side and wait.

Some dogs always have to prove something. Always have something to woof about. That, I guess, works for them.

I'll woof when there is something to woof about. I'm comfortable in my own fur and don't have to stand out in the pack.

Beyond the Biscuit

How do you behave when in a group? Do you have to be the center of attention? Are you able to have a conversation with others? A real conversation where you ask thoughtful questions in order to gain a better understanding of their likes, dislikes, and desires? Or is your conversation filled with a lot of woofing about your accomplishments, likes, dislikes, and desires?

SPECIAL DOGS AND HUMANS

DO YOU THINK SOME PEOPLE ARE MORE IMPORTANT THAN OTHERS, AND THEY SHOULD NOT HAVE TO OBEY RULES?

I've come to learn that some dogs and their humans must be more important than others. You know, real special. Or at least, that is how they behave.

One of the concessions that I have had to make living with Steve and Hoppi requires me to have a leash on whenever we leave our home. I have to do it when we go to the place people *come to stay* and the place people *come to go*. When we visit Dr. Moody or the store with so many yummy pet smells, the leash comes out and goes around my neck. And, especially, when we take our walks around the park or trundle down to the beach. That is where I generally see these very important dogs and humans. Or at least, that is how they behave.

I have heard Steve and his friends speak about something called a *leash law*. Best I can reckon is that it is a rule requiring any dog with a human on a walk to have a leash connected.

On the beach, I often see dogs running after balls their humans throw on the sand. Sometimes the balls are tossed into the water. The dogs go in after them. I think that is called *fetching*. I have never been a real fan of *fetching*. I'll chase after it, but if Steve wants the ball back, he may just have to come and get it himself. But I digress.

I've seen humans sitting in their beach chairs looking at the water, tapping on that thing most humans always carry in their hands, or talking with other humans, while their dogs run around or dig in the sand *sans* leash. (Note: *sans* is French for *without*. Not bad, huh?)

There is a truck that we see on the beach occasionally. When that truck's person sees one of these dogs without a leash, he gets out, writes, and then gives a note to the dog's human. The dog's human then puts a leash on the dog. These two humans never smile at one another. Odd in that the truck's human just gave a gift to the dog's human. Must not be as good as a biscuit.

I've heard the dog's person say things like, "My dog is well-behaved. He does not need a leash. He listens to me when I call him!"

Odd, in that one day I saw one of those so-called well-behaved dogs nip and draw blood from a human. Another day, one went after another canine. Perhaps the humans just did not call them loud enough for the dogs to hear them beckon.

Or maybe the truck's person does not know how important these dogs and their people are. The leash law must not apply to them, but the truck's driver doesn't seem to know that.

Or, at least, that is how they behave.

Beyond the Biscuit

Have you ever noticed how some people believe rules do not apply to them? Why do you think that is the case? Are rules loose like some leashes, loose enough to allow the humans to get out of them when they believe the rules do not apply to them? Do you think some people are more important than others, and they should not have to obey rules? Have you ever decided to behave like the rules did not apply to you?

TINTINNABULATION

WHAT DO YOU DO TO SURROUND YOURSELF WITH SOOTHING SOUNDS?

While humans have an advantage over us canines with their opposable thumbs, they seem to be lacking when it comes to hearing the sounds around us. Perhaps it is because so many of them are so glued to those things in their hands. Or maybe it has something to do with the ear butts some of them wear. Or, just maybe, it is a deficiency on their part. I am not sure. My experiences with Steve, Hoppi, and humans we meet on our walks tells me our canine ears must hear different sounds.

Take Steve for instance. We will be walking through the park on our way to the beach when I will stop dead in my tracks and look off in the distance.

"Come on, Roxie, the beach is this way."

"You mean you cannot hear that? Over there in the bushes? That high-pitched sound? Really? You can't hear that?"

"Roxie, you hear something?"

"That's what I'm trying to tell you."

Eventually, Steve will give a little tug on the leash, and we walk away. Never exploring the sound. Lost opportunity.

On the other hand, I always pay attention to sound. It is something us canines just do. Not only do we hear things humans seem to miss, but we focus on *how* they (the humans) say something.

Consider this example. I've already mentioned how I cannot understand most of what the humans say to one another—or to me. I cock my head or push up my ears or stare intently at times. But it is not so much the words as it is how the humans say the words. Of course, there are a few words that I know. Like *biscuit*. And *kong*. The kong is something Steve stuffs with yummy food. I'll hear him say, "Kong, Roxie, kong!" And then he opens a door on this big box in the room where they keep all their food. And out comes the red kong.

"Yum, yum, yum!" He smiles and is so excited to share this with me. I immediately run to my puppy condo and wait for the treat. It takes me much longer to finish this than a biscuit. And it's worth it.

The point being, besides the yummy stuff inside the kong, Steve's excitement when he says the word connects with me. My tail wags. I drool. I wait for the treat. We have communicated!

There are some humans who mean well, but they can be a little hard on my ears. They speak to me like I hear humans speak to babies. You know, they raise their voices to almost a squeal. Obnoxious. I endure because they smile and are otherwise gentle. But, how would you like it if someone talked to you like that every time you met?

And there are non-human sounds that challenge me. Like Hoppi's red machine with wheels. When I see her with it, I furrow my brow and move to another room. When she connects it to the wall and then rolls it back and forth over the floors, geez, does it ever make a grating sound.

Just like you I am sure, I find some sounds relaxing and enjoyable. Like outside Steve's office and also down in our backyard, where hang tinkling noisemakers that are soothing to my ears. They are made of slender pipes, and when the wind moves them, ahh. The sweet tintinnabulation comforts me. I can listen all day. Sweet music.

Tintinnabulation. It's like biscuits for my ears.

Beyond the Biscuit

First things first. You have to like the word—tintinnabulation—if nothing else. Right? Cool.

What sounds do you find a challenge to listen to, and what soothes your ears and soul?

What do you do to surround yourself with more opportunities for tintinnabulation and fewer harsh and obnoxious sounds?

THE HURRICANE

HOW DO YOU HANDLE THOSE TIMES WHEN YOUR SENSE OF CONTINUITY HAS BEEN CHALLENGED?

I am not one to stress. I have a good life with Steve and Hoppi. I can count on one paw how many times I've felt overly distressed.

Of course, stress happens to the best of us. I've learned that it's part of life. Like when I have to endure those people on top of the boards on top of the wheels or those twerking squirrels in the backyard. I've already woofed about them enough. They raise my cortisol levels. (Yes, *cortisol*. Remember, Hoppi is a nurse. I pay attention.)

I love where I live. With only one exception, I am fortunate to have the run of the house at all times whether Steve and Hoppi are home or not. The exception comes each night when I go into my downstairs doggie condo. Steve says, "Night, Roxie" and then gently closes my condo gate. Kind of like my little gated community. Makes me feel secure. No distress there. My comfort zone.

Most times when I do feel stress, I don't shake, tremble, or whimper. Steve can pick up on other signals that others may miss. Like when my ears go back, or I furrow my brow. Or, I will lay down, head between paws and look at him.

I'm bored. I like where we live but at times it's not overly stimulating. I know all the sniffs and smells here. Let's go for a walk or to the little yellow building or to the park with the cool adult accoutrements. I need to be a dog!

Nothing major, mind you. I get over myself. Especially if we go for a walk where I know, more than likely, a biscuit will be in my future.

There was this one time, though, that I picked up that Hoppi and Steve were the ones feeling some stress. Actually, a lot of stress. And, because of that, I could feel myself get a little wound tight.

They had been watching the moving pictures in the couch room more than usual. Steve would write something on a piece of paper every so often.

"The hurricane is moving." And then he and Hoppi would talk.

I noticed they started putting things in the wrong places. Like furniture from my upstairs deck. They moved that inside the couch-time room. My deck fluff pillow, too. They are usually neat and organized. But now, our house felt cluttered and closed in. Same thing downstairs. The Garnasium did not look like it normally did. Hoppi's car was now sitting where Steve and I did our morning stretches.

All this movement encroached on my dog space. I felt claustrophobic. (This book *really* has helped me expand my vocabulary.) But Steve kept some things as always. Like my food and water were in the same spot, as was my office fluff pillow and my doggie condos. So, that was good. I think humans call that continuity. It helped me feel a bit more in control of my turf and life.

When Steve and I hang at home, I typically stay close by his side. Good energy, you know. But during this time of the hurricane, I found myself following him from room to room more so than usual. That made me feel better. We even took a power nap together in his office, as he had not slept well the night before. In an odd way, I felt like I was helping him calm down and deal with whatever was going on in his human mind. Much like I do when we visit all those people at the place people *come to go* and the place people *come to stay*.

The weather got really windy and wet, so we did not go out for our morning beach walk or afternoon park walk. Instead, Steve walked with me to the backyard. He hoped I would pee or pooh. But I could sense something was different in the air. I stood there looking at the trees moving more than usual. The twerking squirrels were nowhere to be seen. I turned my nose upwards and sniffed. I decided not to venture into the backyard. I would hold my bodily fluids until a better time. I'm nothing if not disciplined.

We ended up staying inside the entire day. Steve would check on the hurricane every so often and then return to his office and tap on those little keypads on his desk. Outside I could see that it got dark, then light; windy, then calm; wet, then not wet. While unfamiliar, this new routine helped keep me calm. As did Steve and Hoppi.

While Steve worked in his office, and Hoppi read, I settled in and did what I do almost as well as sitting for a biscuit.

I slept.

And I felt much better. Of course, when they stopped talking about the hurricane and moved all the things back to their right places around the house, I gave a sigh of relief. We went for a walk. I got an extra biscuit. When we returned home, I roamed my backyard, my domain. Thankful for what I had.

That time of the hurricane threw me because my environment had changed. My comfort zones had been altered. I could feel that Steve was a bit anxious, and that rubbed off on my fur, as well. I felt like I had absorbed some of the anxious energy he was carrying.

I found it difficult to appreciate what had always brought me joy. I did not like the feeling.

Steve, Hoppi, and I were fortunate that our lives quickly returned to what they had been before the hurricane. I hear that some humans and canines were not as blessed as we were.

Beyond the Biscuit

How do you handle times of stress when your sense of continuity has been challenged? Have you found healthy strategies to help you feel more in control even when it feels like all is out of control in your world? Are you able to notice and identify what makes you feel anxious? Who do you turn to—and who can turn to you when they feel distressed?

A LIFE WELL-LIVED

IF YOU COULD WRITE YOUR EULOGY, WHAT WOULD IT INCLUDE? HOW HAS YOUR LIFE TO DATE REFLECTED THIS EULOGY?

Steve and Hoppi have had other dogs. They have photos of them. Every so often they will speak of them. I would like to have met and played with each of them.

Their last canine companion crossed the Rainbow Bridge before I was left on the side of that road at the beginning of my journey. His name was Buddy, and he sounds like he was quite a character. He had personality from what I hear.

While he had short hair like me, Buddy was golden brown in color. He sat closer to the ground than I did. And I hear, like me, he loved biscuit hunting. He and Steve enjoyed sunrises on the beach as well. I thank Buddy for breaking Steve in on these early morning jaunts that have come to mean so much to our lives now.

Buddy handed down another tradition. Many years ago, Hoppi's mother handmade an outfit for Buddy. It looks like a red sweater and has a matching red and white hat that neatly ties around the neck. And a pair of soft horns. The first time Steve brought it out of a box I thought about that hideous red, white, and blue outfit he made me wear on that dreadful Halloween Day.

Oh, no.

"Roxie, Buddy wore this at Christmastime. He would walk with us to each neighbor's house and deliver a little gift. He was our Reindog!"

When he rubbed the red sweater on my fur it felt soft. Much better than that other hideous thing he wrapped me in.

What the heck. Let's give it a go. If Buddy did it, so can I.

Thanks to Buddy, I am the new Reindog. And look pretty darn good if I say so myself.

Buddy was a trailblazer in so many ways for my future appearance. For instance, he was the one who introduced Steve and Hoppi to the little yellow building that I love to visit.

People often ask Steve how long it took to train me. (I really do not like that word, *train*. You *train* a seal. You *bond* with your dog. IMHCO—In My Humble Canine Opinion.) Steve talks about all of the classes, good people, and practice we have had over the years. And, he invariably explains that he is thankful that I have a calm disposition. That's Steve. He gives me more credit than I deserve.

From what I have heard of Buddy and what I sense in our home, I think he lives on through me. I don't know about these things, but maybe he still inhabits our home in one way or another. Buddy, I have heard, lived a life shaped by a dozen core values.

1. Treat and appreciate each experience as if it were the first time!
2. Explore often.
3. Remain curious
4. Smile. Greet. Repeat.
5. Don't miss a meal or a snack.
6. Bark as needed and only when needed.
7. Pull at the leash every so often.

8. Nap as needed. And, often.
9. Enjoy a massage.
10. Unconditionally love.
11. Hold no grudges.
12. Share licks of love as appropriate.

When Buddy arrived at the end of his nearly 105-year journey (in dog years) and readied himself to cross the Rainbow Bridge, his spirit still kept him and Steve and Hoppi going. He had slowed down considerably, but his core values still lived. In his last couple of days, I hear Buddy got to meet and greet his four-legged friends at his favorite renewal hangout (the little yellow building) and spend peaceful time with his family. Steve and Hoppi are forever thankful for the life lessons he taught them. Buddy touched so many that he met on his journey. When it is my time to enjoy the view from the Rainbow Bridge, I hope people will remember me as they do Buddy.

Many lessons learned. Many lessons taught. And a life well-lived.

Beyond the Biscuit

When I look at what I wrote above, I think humans call it a *eulogy*. Words of praise that are offered as an honor and remembrance for a life well-lived.

If you could write your eulogy, what would it include? How has your life to date reflected the eulogy you have just written?

A GOOD DAY TO BE A DOG

WHO ARE THE GOOD PEOPLE IN YOUR LIFE?

I started this book with a nod to gratitude. A lot of beings made my journey possible. For them, and so many more, I say, "Woof!" And there is one more group to recognize.

You, the readers. Thank you for following my journey and sending social media comments and emails to me via Steve. Thank you for taking the time to share your thoughts. While most of us have never met, you have touched me in ways you may never know. So, thank you.

I hope this book has been a reminder that we all must learn to move *beyond the biscuit* and discover the clues, lessons, and growth opportunities that surround us. To do that, as the stories in this book demonstrated, we must pay attention. Perhaps you can continue to share these lessons with the good people in your life.

I hope to have many years left to lead Steve to the beach for our sunrise walks. I look forward to meeting and making new friends wherever we have the opportunity to go. Whenever I join Buddy on the Rainbow Bridge, I want you to know I will stop, look back, wag my tail, and let out a loud "WOOF!" in honor of you.

Allow me to leave you with final story. Appropriately enough, it happened while on the beach.

As Steve and I sat on the sand and watched the sun rise over the water, a neighbor approached and said hello. She looked at me stretched out on the cool soft beach. She smiled and said, "It's a good day to be dog." And then she added, "Every day's a good day to be a dog."

Steve smiled and said, "Especially if there are good people in that dog's life."

Amen.

And thank you for being the good people you are to so many others.

Beyond the Biscuit (One last set of questions before you close this book.)

Who are the good people in your life? What do they do or not do that makes them good? Who would say you are one of the good people in their lives? Why?

~WOOF!~
Love, Roxie

BOOKS IN THE LOFT

Steve and Hoppi have a little loft in our home. You have to climb a steep set of stairs to reach it. In my early days, I would have been terrified. Today, I nimbly amble up those little platforms.

They have put shelves on the walls in the loft. On the shelves, they have a lot of their favorite books. I have seen a few that had canine photos on the covers. I thought you might be interested in them.

Bekoff, Marc and Jessica Pierce. *Unleashing Your Dog: A Field Guide to Giving Your Canine Companion the Best Life Possible.* Novato, California: New World Library, 2019.

Cameron, W. Bruce. *A Dog's Purpose.* New York: A Forge Book (Tom Doherty Associates), 2010; 2016.

McFadden, Judy. *Life with McDuff: Lessons Learned from a Therapy Dog.* Henderson, Nevada: Summit Mountain Publishing, 2010.

Nolan, Hank. *Peter the Drug Dog.* USA: Xlibris Corporation, 2009.

Stein, Garth. *The Art of Racing in the Rain.* New York: Harper, 2009.

Made in the USA
Columbia, SC
19 February 2020

87964227R00098